How to Know the Will of God

by Knofel Staton

You may obtain a 64-page leader's guide and a 32-page activity book to accompany this paperback. Order numbers 40074 and 40075 from Standard Publishing or your local supplier.

New Life
BOOKS ™

A Division of Standard Publishing
Cincinnati, Ohio 45231
No. 40073

Bible versions used in this book:

NAS—*New American Standard Bible* © The Lockman Foundation, 1963.

RSV—*Revised Standard Version* © 1946 and 1952.

NIV—*New International Version* © 1973, New York Bible Society International.

KJV—*King James Version* of 1611.

© 1979, the STANDARD PUBLISHING Company, a division of STANDEX INTERNATIONAL Corporation.

Library of Congress Catalog No. 78-62707
ISBN 0-87239-236-8

Printed in U.S.A.   1979

*Dedicated to
my twin sister
Knova
who has known me
longer than anyone else.*

Table of Contents

The Umbrella of God's Will

"How can a person really know the will of God for his life?" This is probably the most common question that Christians ask. As I travel, I hear it from both mature Christians and new Christians, from both PhD's and high-school dropouts, from both urban and rural residents, from both business executives and laborers, from both whites and blacks, from both professors and students, from both those established in their vocations and those hoping to embark upon careers.

"God, what would You have me to do?" This is a question we ought to ask, for God is concerned with every aspect of our lives. He is interested in everything that concerns us: our worship and work, our choice of a mate. How do we discover God's will?

Categories of God's Will

God is not playing a spiritual hide-and-seek game with us concerning His will for our lives. He does not hide His will to watch us seek it throughout our lifetimes. He has a will for our lives and wants us to know what that will is. There are two categories in His will that we must seek to understand, and we must try not to mesh them together when trying to discern His will.

God has a *revealed* will for all people in a general sense, and an *unrevealed* will for all in specific situations. His revealed will can be called His universal will for us. This category of His will includes His desires for *all* humans. His unrevealed will can be called His particular or specific will for us. This category includes His wishes concerning the numerous specific decisions we must make individually, those that are unique to one's *personal* situations.

These two categories of God's will are similar to the categories of desires that earthly parents have for their children. Parents have a universal will for their children: that is, they wish some things for all their children. These include health, happiness, security, education, etc. Parents also have particular wishes for each child. They do not wish the same specific things for all their children, for they recognize the uniqueness of each child.

Parents do not usually buy identical clothes for all their children (particular will), although they do want all their children to be clothed (universal will). They do not try to influence their children to marry the same person, although they may wish them all to marry. Parents will probably not direct their children into the same vocation, although they want them all to work and to serve. They do not want their children to live with their families in identical homes, but they do want them all to have homes.

As long as Christian principles are maintained, mature Christian parents can be pleased with the vocation, mate, or house each child chooses. One child chooses one specific thing while another child chooses a different one; and parents are happy as long as Christian principles are not violated and as long as their general will for their children is met. Parents are not happy if their children's specific decisions violate their universal (general) will for them. For instance, a child's choice to go naked would violate the universal will of the parents that he be clothed. A child's choice to live with a person outside of marriage would violate a Christian principle and would not please Christian parents. It is much the same with God and His relationship with His children.

God's Universal Will

There are certain things God wishes for all humans (universal will). If we make a choice that violates His universal will for us, there is no way that choice can be pleasing to God. In this category of His will He desires that all persons make the same decisions, and He expects us to know what His will is in these areas.

I used to think God was some kind of fuddy-duddy in the sky, or the bore of the party who could not stand to see anyone having fun. Every time He saw someone enjoying life, as I pictured Him, He would say, "I will take care of that. I will give a new commandment." But this is not God.

God wants us to enjoy life abundantly. He knows what will prevent joy, and He knows what will provide it. Since His will is that we have the abundant life, He provides the Scriptures to share with us how to live that life. He wants our joy to be full. That's what His universal will is all about.

God's Particular or Specific Will

As long as we live within God's universal will, we have freedom to make particular (specific) decisions in our unique situations. Jesus came, among other things, to give us that liberty: "It is for freedom that Christ has set us free. Stand firm, then, and do not let yourselves be burdened again by a yoke of slavery" (Galatians 5:1, NIV). Jesus came to take away the legalism of Judaism. God nailed it to the cross with Jesus (Colossians 2:14).

But the freedom we have in Christ has boundaries. We may think of ourselves as remaining under the umbrella of God's universal will. As long as we stay under that umbrella, we can choose from many alternatives in making our daily decisions. God allows us flexibility as long as we do not violate His revealed will. In giving us that freedom, He honors the fact that we were created as persons with minds, not as puppets with strings. The situation may be illustrated this way:

God's Universal Will
Revealed in Scripture

Specific situations with
individual decisions
to be made

Summary

To determine God's will for our lives, then, is first to discover God's universal will (for all of us) as He revealed it to us in Scripture and in the example of His Son. We must study the Word and believe it—and then make it part of our decision-making process.

8

God's Universal Will

God is not trying to be secretive about His will for us. He is not peeking out from behind Heaven's curtain to see if we have discovered His secrets of how to make the right choices in life. He does not whisper down His will to see if we are being attentive enough to hear Him. He has revealed to us very clearly what His universal will is. He wants us all to know what He desires for each of us, regardless of who we are or where we live.

God has revealed His universal will in the written word of the Scripture. We will be considering all aspects of God's will in the chapters to follow, but in this chapter let us study verses from the written Word in which the Greek word for *will* appears.

Holiness

God desires that all people be holy. "It is God's will that you should be holy" (1 Thessalonians 4:3, NIV). In this verse, *be holy* is referring to sexual purity, as seen by the subsequent explanation:

9

That you should avoid sexual immorality; that each of you should learn to control his own body in a way that is holy and honorable, not in passionate lust like the heathen, who do not know God; and that in this matter no one should wrong his brother or take advantage of him. The Lord will punish men for all such sins, as we have already told you and warned you. For God did not call us to be impure, but to live a holy life (vv. 3-7, NIV).

We do not have to ask about God's will concerning sexual temptation, even though a specific situation may cause us to wonder what we should do. For instance, some suggest that one way to cure a homosexual is to have premarital sex with him. We know that is not God's will.

In his book, *Situation Ethics,* Joseph Fletcher tells of a young lady who wanted help in making a decision. She had been asked to use sex to get information from an enemy, and this information could prove valuable in saving soldiers in Korea, where her brother was stationed. A Christian need not wonder about God's will in such a matter. God's will for all of us excludes immorality.

Being holy includes more than just sexual purity. It includes good conduct of all kinds in the midst of unbelievers. Peter makes it clear that we are not to give evil for evil, slander for slander, or malice for malice: "Be holy, because I am holy" (1 Peter 1:16, NIV); "love one another" (1:22); "rid yourselves of all malice" (2:1); "do not repay evil with evil" (3:9); "seek peace" (3:11).

Salvation

God desires that all people have salvation. Only through salvation can we be equipped to live holy lives. Being sanctified, or made holy, refers not only to right action but also to right equipment. God wants all "to be saved and to come to a knowledge of the truth" (1 Timothy 2:4, NIV). Salvation involves both the acquittal from sin and the equipment of the Holy Spirit. God's presence within us equips us to live holy lives. Paul put it this way: "I no longer live, but Christ lives in me" (Galatians 2:20, NIV). This happens when we live with full trust in Jesus. "The life I live in the body, I live by faith in the Son of God" (2:20, NIV).

Repentance

God desires that all men repent. "He is patient with you, not wanting anyone to perish, but everyone to come to repentance" (2 Peter 3:9, NIV). When faced with the choice of accepting Jesus or not, we do not need to ask, "What is Your will, God?" We need no special experience or right feeling to know the decision God wants us to make.

Inclusion of All in His Family

God wants all ethnic, national, and class groups to be included in His family. This is seen in the phrase *all men* often repeated in the verses pertaining to salvation (John 12:32; Acts 17:30; Romans 5:18; 1 Timothy 2:4; 4:10; Titus 2:11). It is seen in the life of Jesus, and the same truth is evident in the actions of the church in Acts. When deciding about integration in our churches, we need not ask about God's will. His will has been made clear. We know what His will is; the problem is to live according to His will.

Mercy

God wants us all to manifest mercy in our lives (Matthew 9:13; 12:7, NIV). Mercy is kindness, goodness, and a caring attitude. We are to be imitators of God (Ephesians 5:1, NIV).

Thankfulness

God wants us to be thankful. "Give thanks in all circumstances, for this is God's will for you in Christ Jesus" (1 Thessalonians 5:18, NIV). We are not to be thankful for everything, but to be thankful for something in any situation.

Pleasing God

God wants us to be involved in what pleases Him. "For it is God who works in you to will and do what pleases him" (Philippians 2:13, NIV). In this context, this refers to being involved in humble service (2:5-12).

Servants

God wants us all to be His servants. "Like slaves of Christ, doing the will of God from your heart. Serve wholeheartedly, as if you were serving the Lord, not men" (Ephesians 6:6, 7, NIV). Whatever we do we are to honor Him (Colossians 3:17). But our service will be as diverse as our specific abilities (Romans 12:4-8, NIV).

Unity

God wants us to have unity. His purpose is "to bring all things in heaven and on earth together under one head, even Christ" (Ephesians 1:9, 10, NIV). It is God's will that we all be united in Christ and that we live like it. He calls us to "make every effort to keep the unity" (4:3, NIV). To do this we are to be "humble and gentle; be patient, bearing with one another in love" (4:2, NIV). We must speak the truth, use our speech to build each other up instead of tearing each other down, be kind and forgiving, refrain from bitterness and slander, overcome anger, and love one another the way Christ loved us (4:25—5:2, NIV). All these are involved in being imitators of God (5:1, NIV).

In a Nutshell

God's universal will is clearly revealed to us in the commands in the New Testament, and it is under the umbrella of this will that we seek to live. God wants no flexibility among us when we face a decision involving His universal will. And there should be no question in our minds if we know His Word. Now the umbrella looks like this:

God's Universal Will

holiness, salvation, repentance
all men included
mercy, thankfulness
serving and pleasing God
positive and negative commands

Specific situations

Individual decisions to be made

God has revealed His universal will to us, and He expects us to make our own specific decisions with this will in mind. Now we must discover how these individual, personal decisions can be made under the umbrella of His universal will.

chapter

3

Making Specific Decisions

God has not revealed the specific decisions we have to make as we remain within His will. A man cannot look in the index of the Bible under *M* for marriage to find the name of the person he should marry; nor can he look under *L* for location to discover where he is to live; nor can he look under *V* for vocation to discern what career God would have him to follow. We may think life would be easier if decision-making were that simple; but our life would not be as free, abundant, and joyful as God wants it to be.

God does not withhold His blessings from us until we make the one and only decision that fits into His blueprint for us. The idea of one and only acceptable decision in every problem is not found in the New Testament, and neither is the idea of a divine blueprint for every detail of our lives.

God's will for our lives is not like a complete road map that shows us every turn to make. It is more like a compass that gives us the direction in which our lives are to be pointed. Whether you choose to go to college A or college B; whether you choose to serve as a dentist, lawyer, farmer, or housewife; or whether you choose to marry Joe or Bill, you can still remain under the umbrella of God's universal will.

Pleasing God

David wrote, "Take delight in the Lord, and he will give you the desires of your heart" (Psalm 37:4, RSV). This does not mean that God is a Santa Claus, giving us whatever we want; but if a man finds his delight in the Lord, then he will be most delighted when he can give delight to the Lord. And if his purpose in life is to delight God, then he will delight God no matter what profession he chooses.

Delighting the Lord was Jesus' desire. Do you think He gave delight to His Father only after He embarked upon His ministry? No, He delighted the Lord and was within God's will as a child and as a carpenter (Luke 2:52). He certainly was not outside God's will thirty years and within it for only three! He was within God's will both when He was healing people and when He went fishing with the disciples. He pleased God both when He was with the crowds and when He purposely withdrew from them.

I am not less within the will of God when I am sleeping than when I am speaking for Christ. I am not more or less within the will of God when I am teaching at Ozark Bible College than when I was teaching at Lincoln Christian Seminary. Whenever our delight is in the Lord, God is pleased as we live by that affirmation, whatever we do. "And whatever you do, whether in word or deed, do it all [not just one thing] in the name of the Lord Jesus, giving thanks to God the Father through him" (Colossians 3:17, NIV).

We must believe that if we are loving God and living under the umbrella of His universal will, then God is an integral part of our lives. "In all things God works for

15

the good of those who love him, who have been called according to his purpose" (Romans 8:28, NIV). In accordance with God's purpose we became Christians. It is His purpose also to work for our good in all things, not in one thing only.

God is not so small that He can bless us only when we choose one particular alternative among several good ones. Our God is much bigger than that. The bigness of God is what Stephen preached, and what cost him his life. He declared that God cannot be restricted to one land, one building, or one activity (Acts 7). God moves with us and participates with us as we are under His universal will. He travels with us in our decisions. We cannot lock Him into only one choice, and neither does He lock us into one. This means we can make our specific decisions out of faith, love, and hope; not by trying to read a specific blueprint of God that He never drew up.

How Did Jesus Make Decisions?

Jesus knew God's universal will and applied that knowledge to His daily life. Yet He was flexible when making decisions. What was the basis He used to make specific choices? Did He put out a fleece as Gideon had done? Did He flip a coin? Did He pray and wait for a special answer before every action? Did He go into a trance until the answer flashed across His mind? Did He wait for the right feeling? Did He wait for a special vision from Heaven? Did He consult a palm reader or a Ouija board? Did He look for His horoscope in the newspaper? Did He talk with the dead? Did He consult a first-century Jeanne Dixon? Did He flip the Scripture scroll and place His finger on a verse? Did He wait for an inner voice? No. Then what did guide His actions? *The universal will of God.*

In Matthew 5:1, 2 we read that Jesus began teaching. Why? Because He saw the crowds who needed to be taught. That was all the "prodding" He needed, for He knew that God's universal will included edifying others (Romans 14:19).

In Matthew 8:1-4, we read that Jesus healed a leper. Why? Because the leper asked Him to do so. Jesus did not get into a dither over whether to heal or not. He did not put the leper off until He got the right feeling. He knew God's universal will included helping people (Galatians 6:10). He simply said, "I will," and healed the leper.

Matthew 8:14, 15 records that Jesus healed Peter's mother-in-law. What motivated Him to do so? He saw that she was sick. He saw a need and moved to meet that need. He did not go to the mountains to pray about it first, to discover if that was what God wanted Him to do.

Matthew 9:10-13 tells us that Jesus associated with hard-core drop-outs. Why? Because they came to where He was, and He knew that God wanted mercy demonstrated. In Matthew 12:1-8, we see that He allowed His disciples to pick grain on the Sabbath. Why? Because they were hungry. Matthew 12:15 reveals that Jesus withdrew from some people. Why? He knew they wanted to kill Him (verse 14). He used His common sense and decided it was time to get out of there!

As Jesus was facing His weighty decision in Gethsemane, He prayed, "If it be possible, let this cup pass from me" (Matthew 26:39, RSV). If Jesus had acted on the basis of His feelings, He would not have gone to the cross. But He said, "Not my will, but thine, be done" (Luke 22:42, RSV). Jesus knew that God's universal will for Him included a sacrifice—the cross.

This decision conformed to God's universal will, but Jesus had the freedom to make the decision himself. If He had requested them, God would have sent angels to spare Him this agony (Matthew 26:53). Jesus based

His decision upon what He knew God's universal will was. His commitment to God's will took priority over His personal feelings.

We do not have any record to show that Jesus taught people to postpone daily decisions and wait for an answer through a revelation. Rather than encouraging people to pray for "light from Heaven" for daily decisions, Jesus encouraged them to use their intellect to count the cost (Luke 14:28-33). He sharply criticized some of the Jews, even though they prayed often, because their insincerity violated God's universal will (Matthew 6:5-8). Of course we must pray (see chapter six of this book), but not in order to get out from under the responsibility of decision-making. Our first priority is to seek God's kingdom and His righteousness (His universal will), and then not fret over specific decisions (Matthew 6:33).

Jesus had God's Spirit and He knew God's revealed universal will. He committed himself to fulfilling Scripture (Matthew 26:24, Luke 24:27), and thus had peace in His decision-making. That peace can be ours also; but not unless we have His Spirit, and not if we do not know the Scripture. Much of our anxiety in decision-making could be resolved if we would spend more time knowing God's revealed will in Scripture instead of worrying about His unrevealed will.

Flexibility

We must make our specific decisions with faith that God walks with us, instead of wondering if we should have made another choice. God is much bigger than the boxes into which we try to put Him. He can be pleased with whatever we are doing, *providing* we are not violating His universal will.

When making a decision, we need to realize and remember that God is in control of time and history. Since God is Lord of the wider circumstances, situations may change so that the goal we were seeking will not be reached. James said,

> Now listen, you who say, "Today or tomorrow we will go to this or that city, spend a year there, carry on business and make money." Why, you do not even know what will happen tomorrow. What is your life? You are a mist that appears for a little while and then vanishes. Instead, you ought to say, "If it is the Lord's will, we will live and do this or that." As it is, you boast and brag. All such boasting is evil. Anyone, then, who knows the good he ought to do and doesn't do it, sins (James 4:13-17, NIV).

James stressed that we must recognize and accept the universal lordship of God. We do not have to keep saying aloud the words "if the Lord wills," but we are to keep living with that humble attitude. He is Lord over factors that our decisions do not affect, matters in which we are not personally involved.

For three months I had been planning to hold a weekend meeting in Ohio. The weekend came, but the worst blizzard of the century also came! I cannot believe that God covered the Midwest with a crippling snowstorm just to stop me from serving the people in Ohio, but it did stop me. What then? Through all my planning I had recognized that I would speak if God permitted. He did not permit, and I did not speak. My plan was flexible. It could be changed. No decision we make is to be made without recognizing that God is Lord over all. We are not to blame Him or scoff at Him if circumstances do not jell as we plan or wish. We are to be thankful and make the best of the situation.

Paul spoke about his travel plans as if they were God's will, but he had the freedom to change those plans. Twice he wrote that he had changed his intentions. What made him change? Circumstances about which he made intelligent decisions (Romans 1:13; 2 Corinthians 1:15—2:2).

We find a classic example of Paul's flexibility in 2 Corinthians 2:12, 13. Paul was in Ephesus when he learned that the church at Corinth was having difficulty. Concerned about the spiritual progress of its people, he sent Titus to Corinth to teach. He arranged that he and Titus would meet in Troas later for an evangelistic endeavor. At Troas he found an open door (2 Corinthians 2:12). The people were ready for evangelism. But Titus was not there yet. Paul was so concerned about the Christians in Corinth that he left the opportunity in Troas in order to travel on toward Corinth. He might meet Titus on the way and learn more quickly about the Corinthian Christians (verse 13). He knew God would bless him in that decision, and indeed he was blessed when he met Titus with cheering news from Corinth (2 Corinthians 7:5-7).

We also have flexibility in making particular decisions. God does not expect to make all these decisions for us, nor does He want us to run scared because we had ten alternatives and chose alternative A instead of alternative B. God is big enough to go with us and to provide for us wherever we go, as long as we are living within His universal will. Believe this and live abundantly, not anxiously.

Using Our Minds

Sometimes it appears that we want a mindless Christianity, because we look for ways to bypass the power of our minds when making decisions. We may try to make a deal with God or flip a coin. I've done that before. I have said, "OK, God, if the coin flips heads, that is what You want me to do." If the coin did not flip heads, I decided to make it two tries out of three. I was not really looking for God's will at all. I just wanted God's assurance that He was agreeing with what I had already decided to do.

Some people use the "simultaneous experience" approach. I know a man who was praying for God's guidance in choosing a life's mate. While he was pray-ing for this, the telephone rang. It was a girl calling to ask him a question about a school assignment. My friend decided that God was answering his prayer by putting into the girl's mind the idea of telephoning him. He believed that these simultaneous experiences, his praying and her telephoning, were God's doing. My friend immediately started a courtship with the girl, proposed marriage soon afterward, and was crushed later when it became clear that they were not meant for each other at all. He was reading into the experiences what he thought was a special revelation about God's will, but the outcome showed he was mistaken.

Some people feel that their inner convictions help them find God's will. I have a friend who bought a used car in this way. He prayed about needing a car and then bought one because of an "inner feeling" that this was the one God would have him buy. The car turned out to be a "lemon." Should he blame God for his failure to make the right decision?

Others feel that God gives them direction through visions. The mother of an eighteen-month-old baby beheaded her baby because she was convinced that God told her in a vision to do so. Just a few months ago, a minister from Reeds Springs, Missouri, bereft at the death of his mother, was convinced that God told him in a vision that he could raise his mother from the dead. After much publicity and much prayer, his mother was finally buried.

These are bizarre examples; does this mean we should discount all visions? What about the visions in the New Testament? The Greek word for *vision* usually refers to something really seen, not just imagined. Moses and Elijah were actually and personally present on the mountain where Jesus was transfigured, though in some versions their appearance is called a vision (Matthew 17:1-9, KJV, RSV). In all probability Cornelius actually saw an angel communicating with him (Acts 10:3), and so did Paul (Acts 27:23). There is no evidence that such visions were merely dreams, though God has at times used dreams to communicate His will (Matthew 1:20; 2:13, 19).

In the New Testament records it is notable that neither dreams nor visions suggested anything immoral, vulgar, or even egocentric. Neither were the visions just visual scenes; they were accompanied by verbal, audible communication. Regarding visions, then, we must be careful to distinguish reality from imagination, we must not suppose our guess about the meaning is God's revelation, and we must know that God will not tell us to do something that is contrary to His universal will as it is revealed to us in the Bible.

God's Way

God's way for us to discern His will is much more reliable than those I have just mentioned. God has revealed His universal will to us, and He expects us to use our powers of discrimination in the particular decisions we must make daily. Most of our ignorance lies in not knowing and understanding God's universal will, while most of our anxiety comes from trying to determine God's particular will for us. The more clear God's universal will becomes to us, the more we can make specific decisions without anxiety and without guilt or fear of a wrong decision.

God did not create us to function as automatic machines, or to act out of mere instinct as animals do. We were created with the ability to think, rationalize, decipher, weigh, and make intelligent decisions as well as to act on the basis of those decisions. We should be content with our created natures and be thankful for them.

Because we are rational, God's revelation to us is rational. Even His revelation through nature is beamed to our rational minds. Paul wrote,

For what can be known about God is plain to them, because God has shown it to them. Ever since the creation of the world his invisible nature, namely, his eternal power and deity, has been *clearly perceived* in the things that have been made (Romans 1:19, 20, RSV; italics mine).

God's super-revelation in Jesus is also beamed to our rational nature: "No one has ever seen God; the only Son . . . has made him *known*" (John 1:18, RSV; italics mine). God has revealed facts that we can know, understand, and then apply to the situations of our time and culture.

It is true that God revealed detailed instructions in the Old Testament. He had not yet revealed His total will in the person of Jesus (Ephesians 1:9, 10), nor given His Spirit to enable men to apply His universal will (1 Corinthians 2:14, 15).

The New Testament records some occasions when God gave specific instructions (Acts 8:26; 9:1-19; 10:1-6; 16:6-10; 18:9, 10; 27:23, 24). This was not the norm for all of the churches, however. Instead, God inspired people to write epistles to further reveal His universal will. These are to be read and discerned by rational people. The epistles do not call for clairvoyance, but for faith.

Paul called for Christians to obey the truth handed down, not to seek new revelation (2 Timothy 1:13). He even said that the Old Testament history was recorded for our example so we could know what we should and should not do (1 Corinthians 10:1-13). Peter expressed the same idea (1 Peter 1:10-12). So in Old Testament times when God intervened in some situation to give a person specific guidance in making a choice, one purpose was to record for succeeding generations a guideline in making decisions.

OUR Willingness

The New Testament makes it clear that our daily lives are dependent more upon our own willingness to do God's will than upon His intervention to hand-lead us through all our decisions. Jesus even rebuked people for not using their minds to make decisions about spiritual matters, while they were able to make decisions about things of nature (Matthew 16:1-4). The verb *will* or *would* in the New Testament is used often for man's own decision-making, which God expects to be exercised. He will not coerce us into a decision. He expects us to use common sense. Let us look at some examples:

"If you are willing to accept it, he is Elijah who is to come" (Matthew 11:14, RSV).

"Whoever would be great among you must be your servant" (Matthew 20:26, RSV).

" 'How often would I have gathered your children together as a hen gathers her brood under her wings, and you would not!' " (Matthew 23:37, RSV).

In all of these instances, Jesus was giving others the responsibility of using their minds and exercising their God-given freedom of choice.

We find another example of this in the Macedonian Christians who, although deep in poverty, gave liberally to relieve the hunger of their Christian brothers in Judea. Paul recorded that they "gave themselves to the Lord and to us by the *will of God*" (2 Corinthians 8:5; RSV; italics mine.) Did he mean that somehow God coerced them to give? No! Paul prevents this conclusion by first stating, "They gave . . . of their own free will" (verse 3). What is the relationship, then, between "their own free will" and "the will of God"?

These Christians exercised their freedom in making the particular decision of whether or not to give and then the decision of how much to give. They filtered these decisions through the sieve of what they knew was God's will for the hungry. They knew that God cared for the hungry, as demonstrated by the life of Jesus. They knew the truth of Matthew 25:31-46; they knew the apostles taught that feeding the hungry was within God's universal will (Acts 2:44-47; 4:32-37; 6:1-6; James 2:14-18).

With the knowledge of God's universal will, the Macedonians did not need any other special message or revelation. They did what God wants all of us to do. They applied His revealed universal will to the particular situation out of their free and redeemed will. When Christians today understand this and act accordingly, actions will come from hearts of faith, love, and willingness. Then we will really have a loving fellowship with God.

Special Signs

Some people are not satisfied with the simplicity of applying God's universal will to particular situations. There are always those who demand special signs before making decisions. In Bible times, signs were often asked because people did not believe, rather than because they did. What is needed is willingness to obey what we know of God's revealed will, not to rely on signs. This has always been man's need.

Jesus noted that in those very places where He had done most of His miracles the people refused to repent (Matthew 11:20). In fact, He did not trust himself to those who had to have signs (John 2:23-25). Jesus fed five thousand people with only a little bread and a few fish—what a miracle! But the next day when He asked the same crowd to believe in Him, they replied, "What sign do you do, that we may see, and believe you?" (John 6:29, 30, RSV).

Are we any different? If God would come in person and tell us what to do in our daily decisions, it would not make as much difference as many may think it would. You see, He did come in person, in Christ, and many did not believe. Even a person miraculously returning from the dead to tell us what to do would make little difference in our actions. A rich man once asked for that very miracle, but the answer to that request was, "If they do not hear Moses and the prophets, neither will they be convinced if some one should rise from the dead" (Luke 16:31, RSV).

Jesus was saying that we must know God's will as recorded in Scripture, and then apply it to our particular decisions. This is why Jesus spent time teaching Scripture to His disciples. Even after the resurrection, He continued to teach Scripture (Luke 24:27, 44-49). He wants us to understand the Scriptures and to apply God's universal will revealed therein.

Summary

In order for God's revealed will to be applied to our specific decisions, we must be willing to use our minds to apply the Scripture to daily living and then be willing to do what we know is right.

chapter

5

Developing Our Characters

It is not easy to apply God's universal will to our lives, and we cannot do it by ourselves. We need the Holy Spirit to help us (2 Corinthians 3:4-6). God's Spirit in us is God's presence in us, His character within us (Psalms 51:11; 139:7). His Spirit is other-oriented, and therefore He frees us to apply God's universal will in an unselfish way.

To fulfill God's will we need selflessness, not signs. Adam and Eve in the Garden of Eden illustrate this. God spoke to them in person; that certainly was an adequate sign to show them what their decision should be. But they sinned because of selfishness. We must be saved from such selfishness; the Holy Spirit can free us.

Wisdom

The Holy Spirit is called the spirit of wisdom (Ephesians 1:17), and we are to seek His wisdom when making decisions (James 1:5-8). *Wisdom,* as used in the New Testament, does not refer to the accumulation of facts; it refers to moral discernment in applying those facts. Having wisdom is having God's disposition or characteristic within us as motivation and guidance in our decision-making. James 3:13-18 clearly describes the wisdom we need. Using the *Revised Standard Version* and the *King James,* we can make these lists:

Wisdom is not
   jealousy, envy
   selfish ambition, strife
   boasting, lying
   evil works

Wisdom is
   purity, sincerity
   peace, gentleness
   reasonableness
   good works

We may wisely ask the following questions about each specific decision: Is the decision being made without ulterior motives (purely or sincerely), or is selfish ambition or envy a factor? Will the decision bring a peaceable attitude, or will it lead us to "get even" (producing strife)? Will the decision express gentleness? Have you considered counsel (been open to reason), or is the decision made with independent arrogance? Is the decision calculated to elevate self (boasting)? Can the decision be made with integrity and truth, without rationalizing to justify it? Will the decision violate the righteousness of God (be evil)?

In 1 Corinthians 13:4-7 and Galatians 5:22-25 we can find other godly characteristics. If we are wise we will be pure, peaceable, reasonable, honest, patient, trusting, hopeful, fruitful, long-suffering.

Charisma

We must also consider our God-given talents or abilities when making decisions. Every Christian has charisma and is to function in accordance with it, as we see in Romans 12:4-6 and 1 Peter 4:10, 11. In both of these passages the word *gift* represents the Greek word *charisma.* Individuals are like cells in a body, each making its individual contribution to the whole body (Ephesians 4:11-16; 1 Corinthians 12:14-30). Almost any charisma we have can be included under one of the following general headings: preaching, service, teaching, exhorting (strengthening, encouraging), contributing, leading, and doing acts of mercy (Romans 12:6-8). Some of these are very broad categories. There are many kinds of service, many ways of leading, many different acts of mercy.

How do we know what our charisma is? The following guidelines should be considered:

1. Interest. Are you interested in this kind of activity or work? Anything we spend time doing should excite us and hold our interest. Otherwise we will not do it happily and well.

2. Ability. Can you do it? Is it something that you can begin and complete with efficiency and a sense of accomplishment? If so, chances are good that you will do well in this work.

3. Experience. Have you really tried to discover your charisma? Some people say, "I can't do anything," and never really try. This is a cop-out. Sometimes we discover what our charisma is by experimenting and learning (trial and error). In this way we can at least learn what our charisma is not.

At one time I thought I would like to sing in a quartet. So one day in college, when a friend was to lead singing in chapel, I said, "How about putting me on the program to sing a solo?" He did, and I sang "How Great Thou Art." The congregation I was serving asked me to sing a solo, so I sang "How Great Thou Art." Hearing that I had been singing, my mother-in-law asked me to sing for her home church when I came for a visit. I sang "How Great Thou Art."

I stayed in college several more years; I served the congregation for another year; I made several more visits to my mother-in-law's church. No one ever asked me to sing a solo again! I experimented, and learned what my charisma is not.

4. Advice. Listen to what others say. They may see our abilities better than we do. When people tell you, "You would make a good teacher," don't just say, "No, I wouldn't." Consider it.

5. Satisfaction. Do you get personal satisfaction in this kind of service? God does not want us to dislike most of what we do for Him. I used to think that giving my life as a personal sacrifice meant that I had to dislike what I did for God. I couldn't believe that I could enjoy myself and serve God too. How can it be fun to be a sacrifice? How wrong I was!

God wants His follower to be a living sacrifice. He wants us to be excited about our service for Him. He wants us to enjoy living. God has had enough of *dead* sacrifices. The way you present yourself as a living sacrifice (Romans 12:1) is by using your charisma (verse 6). God's charisma for you will mean you will have the time of your life! (For further study, see Standard's *Discovering My Gifts for Service.*)

Seek Counsel

Counsel from others is valuable in making decisions. No person has a monopoly on the Holy Spirit. We are not to be independent of other Christians; we are to be dependent on God and upon each other. Each Christian needs the contribution of other Christians (1 Corinthians 12:7; Romans 12:5). One charisma that some people have is the ability of advising wisely. God often counsels us through others.

The writer of Proverbs said, "Where there is no guidance, a people falls; but in an abundance of counselors there is safety" (11:14, RSV). Either arrogance or a feeling of inferiority may prevent us from seeking counsel. We need to humble ourselves to sit at the feet of others.

Emotions

Feelings are important in making decisions. It is wrong to begin with them, but no less wrong to bypass them entirely. Many people have become miserable because they thought they "should" perform a certain service that they neither desired nor thought they were fitted for.

The Christian is to move from facts to faith to feelings, not from feelings in search of facts. Our feelings should correspond with facts, not overrule them. Many times I have acted upon strong intuitive compulsions, but I can do that with certainty only when I know that my intuitive insight does not violate any known criterion for decision-making. We must not wait for the right feeling before deciding. For instance, we do not provide for our family only when we feel like it. We do not take a sick baby to the doctor only when we feel like it. Likewise we should not give to the church offering only when the feeling seems right. If Jesus had acted on feelings, He would not have gone to the cross. His feelings were saying no, but His faith and commitment were saying yes.

Trust in God

Trusting in God is an all-important factor in decision-making. We must make all our decisions trusting that God will bless us as we walk through any door chosen with the criteria mentioned above. As long as we remain under the umbrella of God's universal will, I doubt that He is as much concerned about *which* door we enter as He is about *why* we choose it. But He wants our trust.

Summary

To determine God's will for our lives, we must allow the Holy Spirit to guide us in developing wisdom (godly characteristics), in determining our charisma, in guiding us to seek counsel, in helping us handle our feelings, and in developing full trust in God.

The umbrella illustrating the process now looks like this:

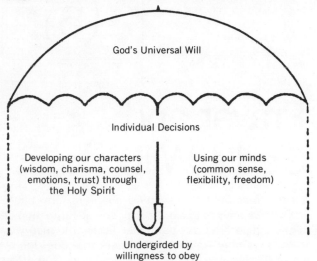

God's Universal Will

Individual Decisions

Developing our characters (wisdom, charisma, counsel, emotions, trust) through the Holy Spirit

Using our minds (common sense, flexibility, freedom)

Undergirded by willingness to obey

The Challenge

As people made in God's image who can enjoy the freedom to which God has called us, let us make our decisions without anxiety. May we not imprison either God or ourselves in boxes that God never intended to exist. The joy of the freedom of decision, the excitement of living out that decision, and the knowledge that God will be pleased with us are blessings of belonging to redeemed humanity.

chapter

6

Prayer and God's Will

After reading the preceding chapters, one might ask, "If we are not to ask God for specific direction or signs concerning our particular decisions, then why should we pray?" I can best answer that question by using illustrations from family life and noting how they are similar to our relationship with God.

Why Pray?

God is our Father; we are His children (as Christians). Communication with our Father is the main way to strengthen our intimate relationship with Him.

Our daughter Rachel is just two years old and is starting to put words together. What do you suppose she says to me when I come home? When I come in the door, her eyes light up, and she opens her arms wide. Then does she say, "Welcome home, professor, author, Knofel Staton"? Oh, no. She comes running and says "Dada! Dada!" She recognizes me in an intimate way and uses the intimate language she knows. She knows me as "Dada," not as author or professor.

As she grows older, she will learn that she can make requests of me and talk to me about anything because I am her father. In fact, this communication will be necessary for her happiness, for she will learn that I do not intend for her independently to map out her own life. Left to herself, I know she would become a human wreck lost in chaos. She will come to realize that I expect her to submit to my will. She will learn to know what I'm thinking, to understand my life-style, and will finally discover what my will for her life is.

My daughter will also learn that I will not give her everything she asks for. Her heart will be sad at times because of my denials; but because of our continued communication and relationship, she will realize that my will involves her own good.

Our relationship with the Heavenly Father is much the same. We can speak to Him intimately (Romans 8:15; *Abba* means *Dada*) and about everything—nothing is off limits when we communicate with God. He expects us to learn to submit to His will. We are to learn that He loves us and knows what is best for us in every circumstance. Through prayer, we will grow to understand His will. We will adopt His values and life-style.

Answers to Prayers

This close family relationship with God does not mean, however, that He will automatically give us whatever we ask or wish for, any more than I will give my children everything they ask for. Some people have read Jesus' words in Mark 11:24 and claimed ahead of time anything they asked of God: "Therefore I tell you, whatever you ask in prayer, believe that you receive it, and you will" (RSV). Jesus did say these words, but He also said many other things about prayer and set limits on what could be received for the asking. In the very next verses, for example, He said that if we do not forgive others when we pray, God will not forgive us (verses 25, 26).

Jesus will not give us control of the world just for the asking. Our prayers must keep our Father's character, mind, life-style, and will in focus. Our own desires are not to be the goal of our prayers unless those desires are ruled by the revealed will and character of God. The more we mature, the more our prayers will reflect God's way of looking at situations and the more we will be able to understand and appreciate His denials.

We will grow to realize that God denies as well as grants. We will learn that some of our requests of God are impossible for Him to grant. They are not impossible because He is weak, but because He is so knowledgeable and good. He knows all the implications of our requests, and out of His desire for our well-being and for the well-being of others, He exercises veto power.

Aren't you glad He is that kind of God? If He weren't, we would actually be our own gods and God would be our errand boy. He is no errand boy; He is the almighty Lord! He has the first and last word (Revelation 1:8); there is nothing for us to add.

Rather than thinking God will give us everything we ask for, I imagine most of us are more guilty of believing too little in the powerful possibility of prayer. Our belief in prayer should rest solely upon our belief in the power and character of God. Paul spoke clearly about that power in Ephesians 3:20, 21. He is a fantastically powerful God who is able to do all that we ask or think. But Paul also said that God is able to do more than we ask or think. He does not just give us what we know we need, but out of His desire for our good He also gives us *above* what we ask.

Paul went even further and said that God can do *abundantly* above all we ask or think. Could anything be greater than that? Yes! Paul said God "is able to do *exceeding* abundantly above all that we ask or think" (Ephesians 3:20, KJV). What a loving Father we have! No wonder Jesus said, "Or do you think that I cannot appeal to My Father, and He will at once put at My disposal more than twelve legions of angels?" (Matthew 26:53, NAS).

How to Pray

Indeed God is able, but Jesus never used prayer for His own advantage. He always used prayer for the fulfillment of God's will on earth. He prayed, "Not as I will, but as thou wilt" (Matthew 26:39, 42, 44, RSV). He was referring to the will of God revealed in the Scriptures (verse 54). He didn't ask for angels to save Him, for He was obedient unto death (Philippians 2:8).

Following Jesus' example, we must pray in accordance with and in fulfillment of God's will. In order to do so, the first step is to be certain that our status is within His will, meaning we must be truly Christians. As Christians, we are in the Spirit and the Spirit is in us; we must pray in the Holy Spirit (Jude 20).

The second step is to develop righteous characters. This was discussed in the preceding chapter.

The third step is to consider the content of our prayers. The New Testament provides us with many guidelines. We should pray for laborers in the harvest (Matthew 9:38), for boldness to speak (Acts 4:29), and for strength to resist temptation (Luke 21:36), not just so we can go to Heaven but also so we can be effective in doing God's will on earth. We should pray for open doors for evangelism (Colossians 4:3) and that God's Word will spread rapidly (2 Thessalonians 3:1). We should pray that governmental leaders will make decisions that will enable us to live in peace and godliness and dignity (1 Timothy 2:1, 2). We should pray for the sick (James 5:13-15) as well as for the safety of God's people (2 Corinthians 1:11; Philippians 1:19; Acts 12:5; Romans 15:30, 31) so that His Word can be continually spread.

Jesus gave us a specific illustration of what we should pray for (Matthew 6:9-13, NAS): "Our Father [a recognition of His kinship to us] who art in heaven [a recognition of His authority over us], hallowed be thy name [an acknowledgment of His worth, superior to all else]. Thy kingdom come [a request that the rule of God triumph over all]; Thy will be done, on earth as it is in heaven [a request that God's purpose be fulfilled here]. Give us this day our daily bread [a request for the necessities, not for selfish indulgence but so we can do God's will]. And forgive us our debts, as we also have forgiven our debtors [this request squares with God's purpose for all—to be forgiven and be forgiving]. And do not lead us into temptation [this squares with God's character; He will not tempt us (James 1:13)], but deliver us from evil [God has designed a way of escape for every temptation (1 Corinthians 10:13)]. For Thine is the kingdom, and the power, and the glory, forever" [a confession that God is in control, not we].

Notice that no phrase in this prayer violates what we know of God's will. It is an unselfish prayer that is concerned about God's plan being accomplished rather than about our pleasures. God was able to accomplish much through Jesus because of the content of His prayers and because of His unselfishness.

Notice how Jesus' prayers were other-oriented. He prayed that Peter's faith would not fail (Luke 22:32), that God would send the Holy Spirit to His apostles (John 14:16), that others might have joy (17:13), be protected (verse 15), be set apart in the truth (verse 17), be sent into a mission (verse 18). He prayed that His people might be one (verses 20, 21). When Jesus did pray for himself, it was so God would be benefitted: "Glorify Thy Son, that the Son may glorify Thee" (John 17:1, NAS).

Paul prayed in the same way Jesus did. He prayed that he would be allowed to help other Christians (1 Thessalonians 3:10, Romans 1:9-11), and that God would fulfill others' every desire for goodness (2 Thessalonians 1:11, 12). He did not pray that their every desire be met, but that their desires for goodness be fulfilled.

Paul prayed that Christians would do no evil (2 Corinthians 13:7), and that their love to others might abound in true knowledge (Philippians 1:9). He prayed for the salvation of others (Romans 10:1), and that the fellowship of faith would accomplish things (Philemon 6). He prayed that others would be filled with knowledge, wisdom, and understanding so they would live lives pleasing to God (Colossians 1:9-12). In short, Paul prayed for the salvation and maturity of others. His prayers were tuned to the purpose of God. No wonder he could be content with either abundance or poverty (Philippians 4:11, 12); he was living not for himself but for God's interests.

And did you notice that "gimme, gimme" did not dominate Jesus' and Paul's prayers? I'm sure they asked for their daily necessities, for they recognized that God was the final source for all their needs and expressed thanks to Him. But they also lived in the assurance that God the Creator (supply source) and God the Father (love source) would take care of them better than He cares for the birds and flowers (Matthew 6:26-30).

The process of achieving this firm trust in God can be illustrated by considering how our children develop trust in us as they grow. At mealtime our little Rachel gets very excited and yells, "Eat, eat!" If we gather around the table and she has not yet been put in her high chair, she gets very upset. She does not yet understand that we are not going to leave her out at mealtime; she thinks she has to beg and plead before she can eat. As her learning is reinforced every day, she will soon know that she is a part of the family and can trust that we will feed her at mealtime. Soon she will no longer ask to eat, but will thank us for the meal.

I find the same thing happening in my relationship with the Heavenly Father. I thank Him continuously for everything I have, even though I do not ask Him for every detailed item. When I ask for my daily necessities, I know that He knows them better than I and will provide for me.

So, to put it in a nutshell, our prayers should be unselfish, other-oriented. They should reflect our trust in God and our knowledge of His will. How many times do we ask God for favors just to benefit ourselves? Sometimes that is why we don't receive what we ask for (James 4:3). We must pray with God's concerns in mind.

I wonder if World War II would have ended earlier if we had prayed not just so our loved ones would return to us (important as that was), but also that pagan nations would see that the God of the Christians was the only God of the universe and that the end of the war would give us the opportunity to evangelize those nations. But that was not our concern. In fact, when General McArthur requested that hundreds of missionaries be sent to Japan, we refused. We were too busy enjoying the luxuries of peace, spending our funds on our own pleasures.

What could happen in decisions of the church if all of us would pray for God's desires to be revealed? What unity we could have if we were praying for God's desires and not our own! There would be no fighting and fussing, because we would not be trying to push through our ideas but would be accepting God's ideas. Only God knows all the implications, and we can trust that He will make all things work together for good (Romans 8:28). God is in us (if we let Him) to will and work for His good pleasure (Philippians 2:13).

Summary

Prayer is the way we maintain our intimate relationship with God; and through its constant use we learn to discern God's will and see things through His eyes. Prayer can be a powerful demonstration that we understand the will of God. It can be a powerful channel through which God works to perform His will in us and through us. Let us labor earnestly for others in our prayers as Epaphras did (Colossians 4:12). Let us trust that the prayers of a righteous man (or woman)—one who seeks God's righteousness and lives it—can accomplish much (James 5:16).

Putting It
All Together

The decision-making process can now be illustrated
in this way:

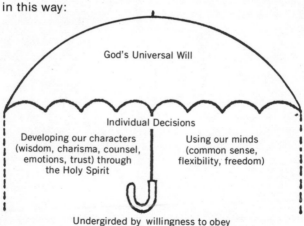

God's Universal Will

Individual Decisions

Developing our characters
(wisdom, charisma, counsel,
emotions, trust) through
the Holy Spirit

Using our minds
(common sense,
flexibility, freedom)

Undergirded by willingness to obey
and unselfish prayers

Now we need to consider how these principles work
out in a practical way with the specific decisions we

must make. Let us explore in detail how some common decisions can be made within God's will.

Whom Should I Marry?

Is marriage within the boundaries of God's *universal will*? Through a study of the Scripture, we find that it is (Genesis 2:24). The Scripture also gives us some general principles concerning marriage that we must consider.

1. Do not marry a non-Christian (2 Corinthians 6:14; 1 Corinthians 7:39).

2. The mate is to be a helper fit for you (Genesis 2:18). Does this person fill in where you lack? Does he bring a balance to your life? Do you complement one another? A person cannot marry everyone who is "nice," but should marry a person who is a balance to selfhood and one whose life he can complement, or complete. The place to begin in choosing a mate is understanding yourself. Can you be completely involved in an interpersonal relationship in which you must give as well as receive?

3. A successful marriage rests upon leaving your parents, cleaving to your mate, and becoming one flesh (Genesis 2:24). Are you ready for these adjustments? Can you cut the apron strings (leaving)? Can you devote yourself to the other so that no interests come between the two of you (cleaving)? Do you share the same life goals and purpose (one flesh)?

4. Are you ready to remain with your mate, come what may, until death separates you? (Romans 7:2, 3; 1 Corinthians 7:39)

Use your *common sense*. Do you really know the person? Have you been through various experiences together? Have you observed the other in his or her home environment? Just saying, "I know this is God's choice for me" is not enough. Neither is it enough to feel like you are in love. You cannot marry everyone

43

you love. I fell in and out of love often during my thirty years as a bachelor.

Is this the *right time* to get married? Will there be other new experiences you must adjust to along with the experience of marriage? These may include a new job, college, relocating, etc. Adjusting in marriage takes time. Will you have the time for it?

Are you using God's *wisdom?* Can you express godly characteristics in your reason for wanting to marry, or in your choice of a mate? Is selfish ambition or retaliation part of the choice? Are you marrying someone because he or she is rich? Is the reason that the mate's talents can aid your personal advancement in some way? Are you selecting a mate out of revenge toward someone who dropped you, or perhaps as rebellion against your parents?

Consider your *charisma.* Does marriage fit your personal talents? (1 Corinthians 7:7-9).

Have you sought *counsel* from others? What do they say about your future mate? What do they advise about the wisdom of marriage at this point in your life?

Consider your *feelings.* How do you really feel about the person? Can you put him or her first? Can you live to please him or her? Are you satisfied with the proposed plans? Is there any feeling of apprehension? Do you really want to get married?

Trust God. Can you marry this person with the assurance that God will bless your union?

Have you *prayed* unselfishly about the matter? Will your marriage mean that you as a couple will advance the cause of Christ? Are you willing to obey God's will in the matter?

What Product Should I Buy?

Some people expect a certain set of circumstances to be present as a sign that God wants them to buy a certain car, house, or sewing machine. God has given us a much better approach.

Is it within God's *universal will* that we own material things? Of course; that is part of the abundant and joyful life He wants for us. The Scripture gives us a guiding principle: Can we own this item without its owning us? Will it detour our love from people to things? (Luke 12:15-21; 1 Timothy 6:10, 11). We are to love people and dominate things.

Use your *common sense.* Will this purchase ruin the budget? Is it needed? Will some necessity of the family be lacking if this is purchased?

Consider God's *wisdom.* Why do you want to purchase this item? Is it out of envy because someone else has one? Is it out of selfish ambition because you want to be better than others? Are you spending luxuriously to retaliate against your mate? What is behind the desire? Is it out of a sense of need and gratitude to God for the possibility of the purchase?

Your *charisma* does not usually affect a purchasing decision, unless the purchase has some relationship to the functioning of your charisma. For instance, your gift of writing has nothing to do with the purchase of a new car, but your charisma for evangelism or visitation may have a bearing upon your choice of a car.

Seek *counsel* from others. Ask them about the brand of item they have and how they rate it. Check out the data in a consumer's magazine. My wife and I were planning to paint the outside of our house. I know absolutely nothing about paint, so before buying any I talked with people who had some experience with paint. I read a consumer's magazine and considered its reports on different brands. Then I waited for a sale on the paint that was best.

We have two cars at home. One has 171,000 miles on it, and the other has nearly as much. A few months ago I came down with "car fever." I decided the kind of car I wanted and the price I was willing to pay. Through a newspaper advertisement, I found a car that I felt had to be the right one. It was a beauty! I did think, however, that it shifted gears a bit funny. Before buying it, I decided to talk to the former owner. He said he had dumped it because of major transmission trouble, and the company could not fix it. If I had not talked to him, I would have bought the car, and perhaps I would have blamed God for the mistake.

Buying on the basis of your *feelings* alone is rather shaky, but there is nothing wrong with buying something you desire as long as the principles of Christianity are not violated. Few people would buy something they could not use and did not want.

Pray that God will give you a clear mind so you can make an intelligent decision.

Should I Change Vocations?

Work is certainly within the boundaries of God's *universal will*. What principles does the Bible offer on this subject?

1. Pay. This may appear materialistic, but it is a valid consideration for a Christian. Let us be honest enough to face it squarely. If the change would prevent meeting the basic needs of the family, do not change jobs. A person who does not provide for his own family has disowned the faith and is worse than an unbeliever (1 Timothy 5:8, RSV).

Make sure you have the true financial picture. Consider your real needs, for you may be able to manage on much less than you have supposed. Of course, do not be unfaithful to the commitments you have made. Your debts must be paid, so you cannot ignore them.

God can provide, but be cautious. Do not make a hasty decision. Do not confuse faith with foolishness.

2. Commitment to your present job. Would the change break a contract or an understood commit-

ment? God wants your word to be your bond (Matthew 5:37).

3. Family considerations. What will moving do to the adjustment of the family members? Are there health factors to consider? How about personal involvements—school and church? What about special needs of family members, such as special education for an exceptional child? What does your family desire?

4. Why do you want the job? For the contribution you could make, or just for the higher pay? God wants us to take pride in our work, not for self-satisfaction but because of its contribution to humanity. "Whatever you do, do your work heartily, as for the Lord rather than for men" (Colossians 3:23, NAS).

Use *common sense*. What will this do to the well-being of the family? What will this do to the schooling of the children? What will this do to the place you are leaving? What will this do to your effectiveness as a servant of God? Is housing available within your means? Will your life-style be changed drastically? Is there a church in that area? If not, what do you plan to do about it? What would your move do to the present congregation or civic organizations you are a part of? Will you be able to train others to take your place?

Consider God's *wisdom*. Will the move or change of vocation express God's characteristics? Is the decision made just for selfish ambition?

Some time ago, I accepted an invitation to become the head of a department in a graduate school. I made my decision with sub-Christian motives. A few years before that invitation came, the same school would not hire me to teach in their undergraduate school because I did not have my doctorate. Now I was asked to teach at a higher level with no doctorate. Why did I decide to accept? I wanted to show them how wrong they were not to hire me the first time! Isn't that childish? A Christian will not be happy deciding on a vocation with such motives—I know.

Consider your *charisma.* Does the new job fit the talents God has given you? If it demands a lot of administrative duties, personal contact, or analytical work, can you do it? I know men who have been very effective in one place but ineffective in another, simply because they tackled jobs that did not match their abilities. Can you use your charisma in the church in the new location?

What kind of *counsel* do you receive from close friends, those who can be objective? You may be torn apart by weighing advice from people who are biased. For instance, someone in the new location may want you to move, while someone in the old location wants you to stay.

Consider your *feelings.* Do you really want to move? Why do you have that feeling? Do not let your decision rest entirely on your feeling or desire. Weigh your feelings against the facts.

Trust God and *pray* about it. Would God approve of this move? If all the other fingers point toward the move, trust that God will bless you in it.

Should I Go to College, or Which One?

Education is within the boundaries of God's *universal will.* Few will disagree about that. There are no Biblical principles for selecting a college, but the Bible is full of principles about proper education. A proper education includes an acquaintance with the world, man, and God. Learning is gleaned from experience, interpersonal communication (formal education), and revelation. Can you find all this at the college you are considering? Or is God "dead" there?

What does your *common sense* tell you? Can you afford to attend this college? Visit the campus and sit in some of the classes. Listen to the teachers. Does the college appeal to you? Are you ready for the discipline? Do you budget your time and money wisely? Can you get along without Mom and Dad? Can you do your own laundry and clean your room? Can you live peaceably with those of diverse personalities and interests?

What would God's *wisdom* dictate? Is your decision based on a prestige image, or upon potential aid to your understanding? Do you want to attend college because of selfish ambition? A poor motive is the advice that used to appear on television, encouraging young people to attend college merely to raise their earning potential. Are you contemplating going just to get away from home? Are you planning to be a "prodigal" son or daughter in college? Can you live for Christ on that campus? Are you inwardly rebelling against college for some reason?

Will the college help equip you to function with your *charisma*? You will not be happy with a college course that does not coincide with your abilities, goals, and interests.

Seek *counsel*. Why not ask alumni, college personnel, and students about the purpose, the personality, the program, the expectations of the college? Discuss your goal with the department head in your major.

What do your *feelings* tell you? Are you afraid to try something new? Understand the reasons for your feelings. Control them, do not let them control you. Attending college requires adjustment, especially if the college is far away from home.

I have a personal friend who entered college to study for the ministry. He had to work to meet the financial demands. During his first semester, an elevator at the place where he worked malfunctioned. When the door opened the elevator was not there, but he had already stepped forward without seeing the hazard. He fell to the bottom of the shaft and the elevator dropped on top of him. He was in and out of hospitals for four years. He will never be able to walk again. If he had allowed the traumatic experience to guide him, he would never have returned to college. Instead, as soon as the doctors would permit it, he was back in college, studying for the ministry. Today he is a chaplain in a mental hospital.

Doors may be shut for you to go to medical school at this time, while a Bible college will accept you; but this is not necessarily a sign God wants you to be a preacher instead of a doctor. There may be other factors to consider.

Trust God to bless you. You may face five possible alternatives (colleges). What does God want you to do? God gives you the freedom to choose the one you want. Choose with thanksgiving that you have a choice, not with fear that you will choose the wrong one.

God wants us to make decisions out of love and faith. He does not want to make all our decisions for us. He wants us to know the joy of decision-making. I learned this when I "put out the fleece" to see if I should go to college to study for the ministry. When the voice on the other end of the telephone said it would not be possible for me to go to college full-time and also earn fifty dollars a week, I put down the receiver and wondered, "How could God answer me that way?" But then I thought, "Who am I to tell God how He has to prove to me ahead of time that He can take care of me?" I knew that I had no motives to be ashamed of. I knew that preaching was within the universal will of God. Why not step out on faith? How could I talk to others about faith if I did not have it myself?

I resigned my job and went to college with a great desire and with faith, not a "fleece." I arrived at the college on a Saturday. I asked for a place to preach on

Sunday. I was sent to Chambersburg, Illinois. After the worship service, a gentleman handed me a check. Can you guess the amount? Yes! Fifty dollars! I continued preaching there until a new preacher was hired. I learned that God could take care of me, that He did not have to prove it in advance.

Pray unselfishly.

Wrong Decisions

Now what do we do if we know we have already made a decision in violation of Christian principles? Remember that God is a forgiving God and can walk with us through a wrong decision as well as a right one. He did this very thing time and time again with the Israelites in the Old Testament. They failed repeatedly. God does not play spiritual monopoly with us so that when we make the wrong choice, He says, "Go to jail."

This does not mean that He approves of our mistaken action, but it means that He has the ability to bring some good out of it if we commit our other decisions to His principles. Admit the bad decision, recognize the wrong principles you used in making the decision, repent of them, and, if possible, change the decision to fit in with God's principles. Above all, remember that God has never been in the business of blessing people who have made only perfect decisions in the past. He is in the forgiving and accepting business. Affirm this fact and accept His acceptance of you, even though you may feel unacceptable.

A Challenge

Let us be willing to make our own decisions. God said through the psalmist, "I will instruct you and teach you the way you should go; I will counsel you with my eye upon you. Be not like a horse or mule, without understanding, which must be curbed with a bit and bridle, else it will not keep with you" (Psalm 32:8, 9, RSV).

God has instructed and taught us through His revelation. He counsels us through the Bible, through the Holy Spirit in us, and through the Holy Spirit in others. He does not want anyone to be like a horse or mule that has to be restrained or led every step of the way.

Let us be willing to study His Word, to obey it, to use our minds and discover the freedom and flexibility we have to make decisions, to seek to develop godly characters, and to pray. Learning to discern takes some growing up, but work at it. We need more Christians who are mature.

chapter
8

God Versus Evil

A car is filled with Christian youth on their way to a church rally. A drunk runs a red light, causing his car to collide with theirs. The drunkard walks away from the accident with barely a scratch, while all the young people are killed.

A baby is born deformed or mentally retarded. In some parts of the country children starve to death, while in other places baby food and formula become outdated on the shelves.

An earthquake, a flood, a fire, or a tornado wipes out both property and people. An airplane crashes and kills hundreds of people. Somewhere there is a war, resulting in many casualties. We read almost daily about members of a whole family being slaughtered in their beds by an intruder.

Our land is beset hourly by personal and impersonal disasters. Why? What or who is behind them? Where is God, if there is one? If there is a God who loves us, how can He sit back and allow such things to happen? What is God's will?

53

Who Is God?

What can we know about God? Can we understand God by studying our experiences, or are we to understand our experiences by studying what God had revealed about himself? This is a crucial question for us who are living among disasters.

To form a picture of God by studying our experiences is to depend upon mere human rationality. To seek to understand our experiences by what we know about God's Word is to depend upon both reason and divine revelation.

In order to affirm the reality and nature of God, we need to consider divine revelation as well as our personal experiences, for God is beyond mere humanity. Without considering and trusting this divine revelation, humans would create their god in their own image. Their god would be no bigger than the thoughts of man.

God says His thoughts are greater than man's: "For my thoughts are not your thoughts, neither are your ways my ways, says the Lord. For as the heavens are higher than the earth, so are my ways higher than your ways and my thoughts than your thoughts" (Isaiah 55:8, 9, RSV). For this reason God has shown himself to man in many ways. The most complete way was the coming of himself in person to earth (John 1:1, 14; Hebrews 1:1—2:9).

The Bible is the record of God's disclosure of himself to mankind, but it is not an impersonal record. It is the Word of God, God's self-disclosure. What a person says reveals his qualities. The Bible is God's speech, thus revealing His qualities.

This is not to conclude that we are to disregard our experiences, but neither are we to interpret God by those experiences. Instead, we are to handle those experiences through a trust in God. Picturing God merely through our experiences will lead to speculation and insecurity. A simple trust in God will lead to understanding, endurance, and maturity of character (Romans 5:3-5; Hebrews 5:8, 9; James 1:2-4; 1 Peter 1:3-9; 4:12-19; 2 Peter 1:3-11).

From God's revelation we know that He is real (Genesis 1:1; Psalm 19:1) and that He can be partially understood by what He has made (Romans 1:20). We know that God is good (Mark 10:18; Psalm 25:8) and all-powerful (Romans 1:20; Genesis 17:1). We know that He is near us (Psalm 46:1; Acts 17:27, 28). He is there to comfort us (2 Corinthians 1:3, 4) and loves us (Romans 8:38, 39).

Evil

Where does evil come from, and how is it related to the will of God?

To say it simply and directly, evil is the result of rebellion against God, not the result of God's direction of people or nature. The fact that God permits evil to exist does not indicate that He planned it or desires it. It is God's desire to bring order out of chaos, not pour chaos into order.

Many Bible students think evil existed before man. Consider the following:

1. There was a tempter in the Garden of Eden, who lured the first woman toward evil (Genesis 3:1-7). The tempter used a lie (evil) to instigate rebellion against God (verse 4).

2. The New Testament speaks of angels who sinned (Jude 6; 2 Peter 2:4). They evidently had the ability to choose; otherwise sin would not have been possible. Angels can hear and speak (Luke 1:18, 19), worship (Hebrews 1:6), observe and learn (1 Peter 1:12), as well as sin.

3. It is believed by some that these angels who sinned form the "principalities" and "powers" that stand in opposition to God (Ephesians 6:12).

4. The leader of these fallen angels is the devil (Matthew 25:41). Jesus affirms that the devil has a kingdom (Matthew 12:26). The devil is called the prince or ruler of demons (Mark 3:22, 23), and the ruler (god) of this world (John 12:31). He is the ultimate source of temptation (Matthew 4:1; John 13:2). His business is to deceive (Revelation 20:7-10) as he did Eve (1 Timothy 2:14). Therefore it is not a shot in the dark to believe that the devil existed before the first human beings, and was involved in their temptation through the disguise of a serpent.

If the devil existed before the first humans, then evil existed prior to man. We read, "The one who practices sin is of the devil; for the devil has sinned from the beginning" (1 John 3:8, NAS). Jesus said, "He was a murderer from the beginning, not holding to the truth, for there is no truth in him" (John 8:44, NIV).

It is possible that the fall of the devil is alluded to in Isaiah 14:12-14 and in Ezekiel 28:12-18. This is not certain, however, because the context makes it clear that the Isaiah passage is describing the king of Babylon and the Ezekiel passage is describing the king of Tyre. At the same time, the language of these descriptions may be attributing to these kings the attitudes and motivations of the devil when he fell.

What is clear from these two descriptions is that man's sin is rooted in arrogance about self and a desire to be as God. That is precisely the temptation Satan presented Eve: "For God knows that when you eat of it your eyes will be opened, and you will be like God, knowing good and evil" (Genesis 3:5, RSV).

Because that is the route of man's sin, we suppose it was the route of the devil's first sin. He tried to be equal with God and perhaps be His replacement; or at least he tried to be God to himself, which would mean autonomy, independence, and individualism. That is why Jesus said of those who opposed Him and of those who would not love Him, "You are of your father the devil, and you want to do the desires of your father" (John 8:44, NAS).

The devil's desire is to stand against God. Jesus called the devil "the enemy" (Matthew 13:39). He is the one who has come down to this earth to turn us away from God (Revelation12:17; Genesis 3:1-7; Job 1). When we sinned, we became God's enemies also (Romans 8:7).

Consequences of Sin (Evil)

There are many consequences of sin or evil. Disasters, calamities, and suffering certainly result from evil. We can place them in two basic categories: personal disasters and impersonal disasters. Personal evils are caused directly by the personal wrongs of people: killing, lying, stealing, adultery, etc. Impersonal calamities are caused by the impersonal forces of nature: earthquakes, tornadoes, fires, sickness, etc.

Let us consider the latter category in detail— impersonal disasters or calamities. God's creation was made with interrelated harmony (ecology). All of nature worked together in God's community of unity. The animals were not a threat to each other or to Adam and Eve. No aspects of nature were in competition; all were in cooperation. There was no sickness or disease.

When one portion of God's creation rebelled, the whole of creation was thrown out of balance. The community (common oneness) was destroyed. Man began to live for self and would even kill to get his own way (Genesis 4). Man went wild, and so did the animals. Vegetation was threatened by weeds and thorns. Diseases came when the perfect balance of God's creation was upset by man's decision.

The Bible makes it clear that all of creation is subject to a bondage of decay and is itself waiting for its

57

liberation from the imbalance. Liberation comes to the whole creation as man lives as a son of God and not as a god himself. (Study Romans 8:18-25.) The harmonizing of creation with its potentially threatening forces depends upon humanity's becoming reconciled to God. That harmonizing and liberation has already begun in the coming of God's new kingdom, but it will not be final until the end, when the rebellious humans will be separated from the obedient ones.

Until that time we will experience both good and bad. As Christians we should be pouring God's kind of life—love, peace, and harmony—into all of our relationships. We are to be as leaven, light, and salt. The consequences affect not just people, but also God's entire creation. God's creation is so closely knit together that all of it feels the results of what is done by the highest earthly creature, man.

Heaven will be heavenly because love will be full. Disasters will not be present because God's creatures will not sever themselves from Him. Our lives will be centered in His Son, not in ourselves. In us who are Christians, that kind of living is invading our earth now. A taste of God's future is seen in man's present.

Both personal and impersonal evils and calamities began when man went His own way, following the lure of Satan. This is not the whole story, however. Not all disasters and suffering are so directly connected to man's sin that we can see the relationship. Read on.

Suffering

Why should calamities and sufferings be facts of life? Why do some people seem to get more than their share? Are our hard times the result of sin in our lives or in the lives of others?

Sin and Suffering

Many of the Jews believed in a direct one-to-one relationship between sin and suffering. Any suffering or tragedy that hit a person was thought to be a direct response from God to that person's own sin. It was necessary, then, to discover what sin or sins were responsible and get rid of them.

This thinking was present in many other cultures. When a poisonous snake fastened itself on Paul's hand, the natives of Malta concluded that it was punishment for a murder Paul must have committed (Acts 28:1-5). In some cultures, this view was worked out in such detail that people thought they could identify the sin a person had committed by the kind of suffering or tragedy he was experiencing.

59

This view of the relationship of sin and suffering raises its ugly head from time to time even within Christianity. When we feel we have been true and loyal to God, sometimes tragedy blows in overnight. We get upset or mad at God and ask, "Why did You do this to me, God? What did I do to deserve this?" Some Christians use the religious rituals and services as a sort of magic spell to keep away suffering. Some persons think that as long as they attend worship services, take Communion, and give their offerings, they should be protected from all harm.

The idea of a direct relationship of sin to suffering is the background of many healing services. A sick person is told that he has sinned and needs to repent and confess his sins. He is promised that healing then will automatically occur. He is taught that all sickness is a curse, but one whose sins are forgiven will not experience that curse because Jesus took the curse upon himself.

Christ's death on the cross certainly did not eliminate all sickness and suffering. It is only when *all* men are reconciled to God that sickness will be eliminated. As long as any sin exists in the world, regardless of who is guilty, there will be sickness and calamities because of the resulting imbalance in nature. Sickness will fall upon the just as well as the unjust.

But it is true that a certain amount of suffering is the direct result of our *personal sins*. God's Word will not be broken. When He says a certain activity is wrong, then engaging in that activity will cause hurtful consequences. Sooner or later these consequences will affect the wrongdoer and perhaps others. The warning is clear in James 3:5, 6:

The tongue is a small part of the body, but it makes great boasts. Consider what a great forest is set on fire by a small spark. The tongue

60

also is a fire, a world of evil among the parts of the body. It corrupts the whole person, sets the whole course of his life on fire, and is itself set on fire by hell (NIV).

But not all the suffering we undergo is the result of our own sins. Some may be the result of *someone else's sin*. An arsonist sets a house afire, and innocent persons are killed. A drunkard kills others in an auto accident. A wife can contract venereal disease because of her husband's sin.

Even some nationwide sufferings result from national or international policies or decisions that violate the principles of God. The problems of economic injustice, famine, and war are often related to decisions that "miss the mark" of God's intentions for earthly living. The Bible clearly says the cause of war is man's selfishness:

What causes fights and quarrels among you? Don't they come from your desires that battle within you? You want something but don't get it. You kill and covet, but you cannot have what you want. You quarrel and fight. You do not have, because you do not ask God. When you ask, you do not receive, because you ask with wrong motives, that you may spend what you get on your pleasures (James 4:1-3, NIV).

God yearns to see the manifestation of His character in our decisions and deeds. He wants to see these not only in man individually, but also nationally and internationally.

Because of the relationship we have with all humanity, we share sin commonly. When a calamity befalls you, you need not suppose it is due to your own guilt, or that you are no longer in Christ.

The apostle Paul knew about suffering firsthand. Much of his suffering was the result of what he was doing. If he had supposed that it resulted from his own sin, he could have concluded that what he was doing was wrong. On the contrary, what he was doing was right. He was preaching the gospel! When he was shipwrecked, he did not take that as a warning not to continue his journey. He was continually in danger. He had trouble sleeping; he suffered from hunger; sometimes he did not have proper clothing (2 Corinthians 11:23-28). All of this suffering was related to sin, but not to Paul's sin. He was the victim, not the sinner.

Some suffering is connected to the errors of others who have no intention of being hurtful. For instance, a person who works just for pay, with no concern for the product, may contribute to careless workmanship. The deficient product may cause a tragedy for others. Negligence on the assembly line may cause a car's brakes to fail, resulting in the death of a whole family. I personally know of a planeload of people who were killed because one bolt in the airplane had been installed upside down.

Some of our present sufferings result from *decisions made generations ago.* The dropping of an atomic bomb in Japan more than thirty years ago is still causing deformity in newborn babies. We are seeing in our young people now the results of the permissiveness of a decade ago. The kind of television shows we allow our small children to watch now will affect their adulthood adjustments. The drug culture will affect many generations to come. Multiple divorces in a family will disturb and distort attitudes and adjustments in the family for generations.

It is not enough to ask what God's will is concerning suffering and tragedies. We must also ask, "What is man's responsibility, individually and corporately?" At the same time, we cannot connect every suffering with a corresponding sin. The disciples tried to do that when they asked Jesus, "Who sinned, this man or his parents, that he was born blind?" (John 9:2, NIV). Jesus answered, "Neither."

It is also a mistake to conclude that those who suffer more severely are worse sinners. Jesus countered this idea:

> Do you think that these Galileans were worse sinners than all the other Galileans because they suffered this way? I tell you, no! But unless you repent, you too will all perish. Or those eighteen who died when the tower in Siloam fell on them—do you think they were more guilty than all the others living in Jerusalem? I tell you, no! (Luke 13:2-5, NIV).

True, there are certain clear-cut consequences that we call upon ourselves by the decisions we make. But often these are the result of simply failing to use our common sense, and it is not correct to blame God for them or associate them with sin.

Laws of Nature and Suffering

God has created a marvelous world in which He has programmed many laws of nature. These laws are constant. We can and do depend upon them. Without them we could make no plans. God has built into these laws both blessings and wrath. We are blessed when we live in accordance with the laws, but we experience wrath when we violate them. Some of what the Bible refers to as the wrath of God comes in the package with violation of His natural laws.

The law of gravitation is a blessing, and we depend upon it. We could not build an airplane or a car without depending upon it. We could not put anything on the table without it. A person certainly couldn't wear a wig without it! But the law of gravitation becomes wrath when someone falls off a high place. Such a tragedy is not connected with a personal sin. A baby falls out of a crib and sustains a serious injury, but we cannot blame God. We can expect to be hurt when a law of nature is violated, and ignorance of that law makes no difference in the results.

Sufferings are caused also by a combination of sin and violation of the laws of nature. A drunkard (sin) causes an automobile collision (violating law of nature). A person with uncontrolled anger (sin) uses a gun to shoot another person (violating law of nature). Sin seems to find ways to do both—violate the laws of nature and cause suffering.

It is possible that diseases also are related to violation of the laws of nature. We do not know the exact cause of many diseases, but it is my judgment that they are caused by a lack of harmony within nature. The lack of harmony is caused by the decisions of men. However, the total creation is so vast and complex that it is impossible to pinpoint with certainty a specific cause of a specific disease. We do know that there is a complex interdependence between man and nature. What could be causing the cancer we see all about us? Is it food that we are eating? Drugs we are taking? Could it be the sprays that we use on crops? Is it something we are doing now, or can it be something that was done or begun a generation or two before us? The answer is indeed complex. Blaming God is not the answer.

The Mind and Suffering

Some suffering is caused by personal sin, by the sin of another, by the mistakes of someone else, or by violating the laws of nature. But apart from this, much suffering is caused by our own attitudes and thoughts about God, ourselves, others, and life itself. This type of suffering is called psychosomatic. It is no longer a secret that many people are sick because they think they are. It has been estimated that somewhere between seventy and ninety percent of all sicknesses have their source in the mind.

The Bible makes it clear that our speech affects our health:

> There is one whose rash words are like sword thrusts, but the tongue of the wise brings healing (Proverbs 12:18, RSV).

> Pleasant words are like a honeycomb, sweetness to the soul and health to the body (Proverbs 16:24, RSV).

> Death and life are in the power of the tongue (Proverbs 18:21, RSV).

> Anxiety in a man's heart weighs him down, but a good word makes him glad (Proverbs 12:25, RSV).

> A gentle tongue is a tree of life, but perverseness in it breaks the spirit (Proverbs 15:4, RSV).

The Bible also says our attitudes affect our health: "A man who is kind benefits himself, but a cruel man hurts himself" (Proverbs 11:17, RSV). "A tranquil mind gives life to the flesh, but passion makes the bones rot" (Proverbs 14:30, RSV).

Perhaps far more than we imagine or suspect, sickness and suffering result from our being out of harmony with God, ourselves, and others. Anxiety and anger take a great toll. God's direction for our lives has far-reaching implications, calling for selflessness, trust, love, peace, and a reordering of values. God does not give us directions just to get us to Heaven. He also wants to bring some of the Heavenly life-style into our earthly existence, so that we may have abundant living.

Some doctors have suggested that medical bills among Christians could be cut at least in half, if the Christians would exercise love and fellowship with each other more. The Bible makes it clear that Christian fellowship is needed for our joy to be complete (1 John 1:1-4, 7), and joy affects our health. The Bible says that our fellowship is partly for the purpose of encouraging one another, building up one another, and cheering up one another (1 Corinthians 14:3; Hebrews 10:25). We should live with one another in kindness, gentleness, patience, forgiveness, and love, binding everything together in harmony (Colossians 3:12-16); and the reason is no mystery. These qualities are needed if people are to have fellowship. As a matter of fact, factions within the church can be the cause of physical sickness and death (1 Corinthians 11:17-30).

Surely the devil is personally involved in luring us to sin and causing suffering. But why does God allow the devil to do so? Where is God and what is He doing in the midst of these calamities, while we are facing suffering and tragedy? What is His will? The next chapter will consider these questions.

Where Is God?

"God, where are You? We are hurting!" That is not a new cry for people who have put their trust in a God of love. It has been heard many times throughout history ancient and modern.

God's Presence

Toward the end of the first century, when it looked as though everything was falling in on the Christians, God heard that same cry. Persecution was severe. Some Christians were deported (Revelation 1:9), some were put in dungeons (2:10), and others were killed (20:4). In addition to this attack on the Christians, there were the natural calamities of hunger and disease (6:8; 7:16). As if that were not enough, within the church itself there were false teachers causing internal problems (2:2, 14, 20, 24). The Christians were asking, "Where is our future? Where are You, God? Don't You care? What about all those promises you made to us: 'I'll never desert you'; 'All things work to the good'; 'You will be more than conquerors'? Why, God?"

The book of Revelation shows us clearly that God and Christ know all about our problems, and they care. John had a wonderful vision of Christ as well as a vision of all the problems surrounding God's people. Where was Christ? He was in the midst of the people with the problems (1:13). "I'm there in the suffering with you" is our assurance.

John saw Christ clothed with a long robe and a golden girdle—the symbols of authority. Although it appears that suffering, pain, and tragedy may have the last word, they do not. Jesus Christ is on His throne. The future belongs to Him. There is no need to be afraid, for He is the first and the last (1:17). After all the smoke has cleared, Jesus will still be there in the midst of His people. To John, Jesus' feet were as burnished bronze (1:15), a symbol of stability. Nothing will knock Him off His throne. He is secure. "Behold I am alive for evermore, and I have the keys of Death and Hades" (1:18, RSV).

What does it mean to say that Jesus is "with us" in our suffering? For one thing, it means He suffers with us. We have, as Christians, a personal relationship of oneness with Him. The church is called the body of Christ, and Jesus is called the head of the body (Ephesians 1:22, 23). When the body hurts, so does the head. Our sufferings are Christ's sufferings, as His are to be ours (2 Corinthians 1:5; 1 Peter 4:13).

He is also with us so that we have access to His strength. His resources are ours. Because He is the almighty one, we can be more than conquerors over whatever threatens us (Romans 8:37). "For God did not give us a spirit of timidity but a spirit of power and love and self-control" (2 Timothy 1:7, RSV). Never are power and self-restraint more necessary than in the face of difficulty. The nearness of God is not determined by our feelings. We know He is there because He promised to be there, and He is faithful to His promises whether we "feel" He is there or not. We should train our feelings to match the facts, not imagine the facts must match our feelings.

The Impartiality of God

The Christian need not worry and say, "What have I done to deserve this?" God does not use suffering, pain, and tragedy to "get even" with us for wrongdoing, although God may utilize these situations to discipline us (2 Corinthians 12:7-10; 1 Corinthians 11:32). We have seen already that a person may suffer as a result of the following: his own sin, violating the consistent laws of nature, someone's unintentional mistakes, or someone else's sin. The latter two of these often bring suffering to people who do not deserve it at all.

Nature itself has experienced an upheaval because of man's sin, and man in return receives the consequences of that upheaval. God does not normally intervene to isolate His people from these natural consequences, although He has done so at times. "God is no respecter of persons": that is, He is not partial. The sun shines upon all, both good and evil, and the rain falls upon all, both good and evil. Either rain or sunshine can be harmful as well as helpful. Likewise impartial are natural disasters such as tornadoes, famines, and disease, whether it be a little headache or terminal cancer. To be "in Christ" is no guarantee that we will escape crises and calamities. They will exist as long as the tempter is still alive and active among us.

God's Goodness

The goodness of God in the midst of our pain is apparent. First, pain in itself is a blessing from God. It is the warning that something is wrong. Without the gift of pain, we would not take our hands out of the fire until too late. Without pain one might lose the use of all the members of his body by misusing or neglecting them. But this does not make pain comfortable; it still hurts.

Pain is also limited and temporary. It can go only so far before our senses become numb to it. Because of God's goodness, our bodies are mortal; thus the pain in them is temporary. God will not let pain and suffering have the last word. Physical death is a God-given relief from earthly pain and pressures.

Not only has God provided an exit from earthly pain, but He has also provided an escape from eternal pain and suffering. He accomplished this in the death and resurrection of Jesus Christ. Jesus experienced for us the eternal consequences of sin. He took separation from the Father in our stead. "Surely he bore our griefs and carried our sorrows; . . . the chastening for our iniquities fell upon Him for our well-being, and with His stripes we are healed" (Isaiah 53:4, 5, author's paraphrase). Our well-being and healing are both spiritual and physical. Although the blessings begin in this life, they do not reach their fullness until that time when the perishable puts on the imperishable and the mortal puts on the immortal (1 Corinthians 15:53).

God's Permission

If God is good, then why does God permit the devil to lure us into being enemies of God? The answer lies in the love of God. Sounds strange, doesn't it?

Because of God's love He created us and allowed us to participate in His own image. Since God is love (1 John 4:16), he gave man the capacity to love. Man and woman were made with the ability to love God and to love each other. In order to express that love fully, there must be an alternative. God wants us to fellowship with Him, not because we have no other choice, but because it is our choice. God will not force man to love Him. Love does not work that way. Love woos and waits; love permits the other the freedom to respond out of a desire to do so.

In the Garden of Eden, God wanted man to remain in the community of unity; however, he provided an alternative. That alternative was the one forbidden tree. To eat from it would be disobedience, and disobedience would break the ideal fellowship, the community. When Adam and Eve chose that alternative they hid from God (Genesis 3:8), and they had to leave the garden and be separated from God (Genesis 3:24).

We often call the tree of the knowledge of good and evil man's first temptation, but I prefer to call it man's grand opportunity. As long as Adam and Eve did not partake of the tree, they were saying to God, "Father, we are here because we want to be and because we love You, not because we have to be here." They had the opportunity to show that attitude and preserve their fellowship with God. But their sin broke the community of unity, for the attitude behind the sin was an anti-community attitude. Sin is a turning to our own way. "All we like sheep have gone astray; we have turned every one to his own way" (Isaiah 53:6, RSV). Individualism destroys the community.

God's love permitted the temptation because out of His love He made us in His own image. We are persons, not puppets. God could have made us as heavenly robots, but He did not. That was God's calculated risk. Out of true love He gave His gift of freedom. He did not force the one and only decision on man, but He did force man to the position of making a choice.

Yes, God is here and cares; but the devil is also here. How does God deal with him? Read on.

chapter

11

Victory
Over Satan

Satan Is at Work

Sin continues, partly because the tempter is still active and partly because people continue to yield to him. The death and resurrection of Jesus did indeed defeat Satan, but he will not be finally crushed until the second coming of Christ. Although God's kingdom has come, Satan's kingdom has not departed. We are living in the overlapping of the kingdoms.

The church is at war with Satan's principalities and powers (Ephesians 6:12). Although Jesus has already defeated Satan, the battle goes on. Satan is like a defeated general who will not admit defeat. He is still prowling "like a roaring lion, seeking some one to devour" (1 Peter 5:8, RSV).

Satan is trying to defeat us on at least three battlefronts. We need to be alert and ready to resist all of his attacks with vigor and determination.

1. He wants us to believe that all sickness, suffering, and tragedy are the result of demon possession. If he can get us hooked on that idea, then he will get us

to substitute exorcism (casting out demons) for repentance, a life of loving fellowship, and edification. If we are fooled by this lie of Satan, we will spend more time looking at our crisis than at Christ. We will spend more time exorcising than evangelizing. Satan knows that in evangelism lies his defeat, so he tries to divert our attention to some effort that will be less disastrous to him.

2. Satan wants us to believe that our personal plights are the result of our lack of spirituality. If Satan can get us to believe that, he can get us to doubt our status in Christ. He delights in getting us to think that the prayer of faith will always heal the sick. Then when healing does not take place, we doubt either our own faith or the faith of the church. What a masterful way to program disillusionment!

Satan is tickled beyond words when a Christian takes a verse of Scripture out of context, such as "If two of you agree on earth about anything they ask, it will be done for them by my Father in heaven" (Matthew 18:19, RSV). So what happens when two people agree that another should get well, and he does not? Doubt comes. Other verses likewise can be isolated and misused: "Whatever you ask in my name, I will do it" (John 14:13, RSV). "If you abide in me, and my words abide in you, ask whatever you will, and it shall be done for you" (John 15:7, RSV). When we ask and healing does not take place, or when disaster comes in spite of our prayers, we begin to doubt either Christ's power or our relationship with Him. Another victory for Satan!

Look again at the first quoted verse in the preceding paragraph. Consider it with its context, Matthew 18:15-35. Then it becomes plain that verse 19 refers to praying for God's will to be done in the matter of disciplining a brother. Verse 19 says the people praying must be in agreement; but note also that their agreement must be in accordance with God's agreement as stated in verse 18: "Whatever you bind on earth shall be bound in heaven, and whatever you loose on earth shall be loosed in heaven" (RSV).

Verse 18 also needs careful study. Binding or loosing means accepting or rejecting the person who has done wrong, and whether he is accepted or not depends on whether he repents of his wrong or not. The original Greek does not read "shall be loosed in heaven." It reads "shall have been loosed." The idea is that the disciples should accept or reject on earth what already has been accepted or rejected in Heaven. That is, our prayers should be for what God has already decided.

John 14:13 likewise is not a blanket promise to grant just any request we may make. It refers to prayers asking God to use us in His work (verse 12), and it refers only to what we ask in Jesus' name. Asking in Jesus' name does not mean repeating those words at the end of a prayer. It means asking for what Jesus wants rather than for what we want.

The promise of John 15:7 is limited in a similar way. It has to do with prayers for fruitfulness (verses 5, 8), and it does not apply unless we are living in Christ and guided by His word (verse 7).

None of these verses can properly be taken as a promise that God will always heal us or end our suffering because we ask Him to.

Suffering does not indicate a lack of spirituality, or a lack of power in our prayers. Jesus experienced severe pain, and that was not His only suffering. He suffered mental and emotional anguish as well as pain. Would anyone suggest He lacked spirituality or that He did not pray as He ought? (See 1 Peter 2:20-24.)

Paul also suffered much (2 Corinthians 11:23-29). Three times he prayed that a thorn in his flesh be taken from him, but it was not (2 Corinthians 12:7-9).

He knew what it meant to be sick (Galatians 4:13). Does that indicate that he was not spiritual enough to pray effectively for healing? Or does it indicate rather that God does not always choose to heal the sick even when a godly man requests it?

Stephen became a martyr (Acts 7:59, 60), though we are told that he was "full of faith and the Holy Spirit" (Acts 6:5). Epaphroditus got sick doing the Lord's work (Philippians 2:25-30); Timothy had stomach trouble (1 Timothy 5:23). Paul left Trophimus ill at Miletus (2 Timothy 4:20). Does that mean their prayers were faulty, or that any promise of God was broken?

Ancient tradition tells of other suffering that is not recorded in Scripture. It is said that Matthew was killed with a sword in Ethiopia; Mark was dragged in the streets in Alexandria; Luke was hanged in Greece. John was put in boiling oil, but survived. Peter was crucified upside down; Philip was hanged; Bartholomew was flayed; Andrew was bound to a cross and died there while preaching. Thomas was thrust through with a sword in India; Matthias was stoned and then beheaded. Barnabas was stoned; Paul was beheaded. Would we want to use these Scriptures—Matthew 18:19; John 14:13; 15:7—against them as spiritual leaders?

God never promised that spiritual people would be guarded against suffering. Not once did God promise that. Instead, He promised that we would be blessed *in* our suffering (Matthew 5:10-12; 2 Corinthians 1:6; Philippians 1:29; 3:10; 1 Thessalonians 2:14, 15; 2 Timothy 2:12; 3:12; James 5:10, 11; 1 Peter 1:3-9; 2:19-24; 3:14-22; 4:1, 2, 12-19; 5:10).

3. The third way Satan is trying to defeat us is by tempting us to do evil. When we yield, we pour alienation into God's system. We set person against God, person against person, person against nature, and nature against person.

Satan is shrewd. He uses both the world God created and the desire God gave us as his arena of temptation. James put it this way:

> Let no one say when he is tempted, "I am tempted by God"; for God cannot be tempted with evil and he himself tempts no one; but each person is tempted when he is lured and enticed by his own desire. Then desire when it has conceived gives birth to sin; and sin when it is full-grown brings forth death (James 1:13-15, RSV).

The devil uses our desires to lure and entice us. What a trick! Our basic desires—hunger, thirst, sex, self-preservation, etc.—are God-given and not bad in themselves. To satisfy those natural desires, God gave us a very good world within which those desires could be met. He gave us food to meet the desire for hunger, liquid for thirst, males and females for sex. But because God not only loves us but knows us, He also gave commands concerning these desires. His commands serve as guardrails to protect us along the highway of life. As long as we remain within the guardrails, we can enjoy our earthly journey. He gave us the important guardrail of moderation to guide our eating and drinking. He provided marriage as a guardrail to our enjoyment of sex.

Satan uses the same desires and the same world, but lures and entices us to satisfy our desires beyond God's guardrails. He says, "Eat and drink all you want. Use things just for yourself." Satan baits the hook and it looks good. We fail to see the hook inside the bait.

Satan treats us like dumb creatures. The words "lure" and "entice" are hunting and fishing terms. Christians must refuse to be caught like animals that are governed by appetite! We are made in God's image and should act like it.

The Victorious One

In the face of both temptations to evil and the sufferings of life, we must realize that over against Satan is God. He still has the last word, and His promise to us is this: "No temptation has overtaken you that is not common to man. God is faithful, and He will not let you be tempted beyond your strength, but with the temptation will also provide the way of escape, that you may be able to endure it" (1 Corinthians 10:13, RSV). Satan is like a lion on a chain, but God is holding the chain. God will never allow a temptation we cannot overcome.

I am confident that each day Satan tries to tempt me beyond my ability, but God says, "No!" Satan then tries again a bit closer to my level of maturity, but God still says, "No!" Those temptations are never permitted to enter my mind. Finally Satan gets down to my level of maturity, and God says, "OK, you can use that, Satan, because he is able in his present maturity to handle that one." That temptation enters my thinking or experience. The moment it does, I know that I (living in Christ and allowing Christ to live through me) am bigger than the temptation; otherwise God would not have allowed the thought or situation to arise. When I yield to the temptation, I have permitted something weaker than myself to be victorious over me.

Satan is always weaker than the Christian. "He who is in you is greater than he who is in the world" (1 John 4:4, RSV). God will not keep all temptation and suffering away from us, but He will not let us be touched by any that are more powerful than we (Job 1). What a promise!

77

chapter 12

Progress

Pain, sickness, and suffering are not a part of God's intention for mankind. That is clear when we consider life in the Garden of Eden before the fall. We can also see this as we read about the activity of Jesus, who healed sicknesses and was full of compassion, and when we view Heaven with John:

> He shall wipe away every tear from their eyes; and there shall no longer be any death; there shall no longer be any mourning, or crying, or pain; the first things have passed away. And He who sits on the throne said, "Behold, I am making all things new" (Revelation 21:4, 5, NAS).

God allows the built-in penalty of sin to sting, the imbalance of nature to hurt, and the schemes of Satan to test; but God has the first and last word. The first word is His permission based upon our maturity. The last word is the good that He can work through any situation. While Satan intends to use certain circumstances to embitter us, God intends to use those same circumstances to better us. And we ourselves cooperate with Satan or with God to bring about one result or the other.

Paul affirmed that truth when he said, "And we know that in all things God works for the good of those who love him" (Romans 8:28, NIV). What a promise! Circumstances are never without the accompanying activity of God, who is working them into good, regardless of the evil intentions of the powers behind those circumstances.

Progress in Faith

We may ask, "What good is God working?" No single answer can be given, for each different situation may result in a different good. But we can note some general principles. James says, "Consider it all joy ... when you encounter various trials, knowing that the testing of your faith produces endurance" (James 1:2, 3, NAS). The word *testing* used in this instance is a term used to describe the refining of precious metals through fire. Going through the fire is of benefit to the metal, for the fire burns off the dross, the inferior materials that are found in the ore but are not part of the metal. It is the same when our faith hits the fire of testing. Through suffering our faith comes out stronger and purer because the sham and counterfeit have been burned off.

Progress in Evaluation

Suffering situations have a way of enabling us to separate what is temporary from what is eternal. Sickness reminds us that we are all temporary. Natural calamities (earthquakes, tornadoes) remind us that property and possessions are temporary. To find security or stability in disaster, our eyes turn to what is lasting—God. He will never blow away or die. God does not make suffering happen, but He does turn it to good use. The apostle Peter put it this way to his Christian brethren:

> Now for a little while you may have suffered grief in all kinds of trials. These have come so that your faith—of greater worth than gold, which perishes even though refined by fire—may be proved genuine and may result in praise, glory, and honor when Jesus Christ is revealed (1 Peter 1:6, 7, NIV).

Progress in Maturity

God also uses suffering situations to help us grow and mature spiritually. We may mature without them, of course, but God uses the situations to speed our maturity. James said, "The testing (refining) of your faith produces endurance" (James 1:3, NAS). *Endurance* refers to remaining under or standing firm in a difficult situation, and such endurance or perseverance produces character (Romans 5:4). Character, personal maturity, and increased trust are never gained by running away from tough circumstances or ignoring them. How can we measure our maturity with God if we do not walk through difficult times with Him? How can we grow if we always look for the nearest exit?

Whenever we come upon a distressing situation, we are tempted to avoid growth by putting up one or more defense mechanisms. A defense mechanism is a tool we use to avoid facing a problem squarely and handling the difficult situation. There are two broad categories of defense mechanisms: passive and violent. Both of these dodge responsible involvement.

To illustrate the passive defense mechanism, let us examine a common happening in marital conflict. A husband and wife are not getting along well, and one partner decides to take the passive role. This can be done by using the silent treatment (refusing to talk about the problem), or taking an exit (getting out of the situation by separation or divorce). Neither of these passive roles will add to one's understanding or growth. Both bypass responsibility and fail to help the person involved to grow toward maturity.

Sometimes the silent treatment is used in situations other than marital trouble. A person refuses to discuss his problem with anyone. Then his imagination goes to work and builds the difficulty up out of proportion. He withdraws into himself and does not mature. Others exit from their troubles by resigning from a job, moving out of town, or committing suicide. They cannot grow to maturity by any of these routes.

In using the violent defense mechanism, one may lash out at another person with either his lips (verbal) or his limbs (physical). Most people especially like to use this violent approach when they have been treated wrongly, for it seems to soothe their hurt feelings. But to use this is to bypass meaningful interpersonal relationships with others. It feeds the narrowness of the selfish ego.

Both the passive and the violent mechanisms mean that the person draws only from his own emotional resources. He allows his life to rotate around self. His values are centered in his ego, and he will not mature beyond his present level of selfishness.

In contrast, Jesus showed us how to handle mistreatment. He endured it: He remained under it with trust in God. After considering Jesus' example, Peter said, "To this you have been called, because Christ also suffered for you, leaving you an example, that you should follow in his steps" (1 Peter 2:21, RSV).

What was that example? He committed no sin. No deceit was found in His mouth. When He was reviled,

He did not revile in return. While under suffering, he uttered no threats. What did He do then? He kept trusting himself to God, who judges righteously. He demonstrated the endurance of faith (1 Peter 2:22, 23). He maintained His fellowship and interpersonal exchange with others. He differed, but without animosity.

This is not an easy example to follow, but as we learn to follow it we grow spiritually. The testing produces endurance, which in turn produces a mature and stable character. Peter suggests that godliness, brotherly kindness, and love are included in this character (2 Peter 1:7). This is what Paul meant when he said, "We also rejoice in our sufferings, because we know that suffering produces perseverance; perseverance, character; and character, hope" (Romans 5:3, 4, NIV).

The word for *character* is from the same Greek root as that of *testing.* Character comes out of testing. Is it possible that without testing there is little development of character? It is interesting to note that the Greek word for *glory* also comes from the same word family as *testing* and *character.* Can it be possible that, after becoming Christians, we do not mature from one degree of glory to another if we use defense mechanisms to avoid difficult situations? Paul says that by beholding the glory of the Lord we all "are being changed into his likeness from one degree of glory to another" (2 Corinthians 3:18, RSV): that is, we are progressing from our own character to His. We do that as we behold and learn and follow His way of living through difficult times.

Immediately following these words, Paul affirms that he will not bypass difficulties that may come from being a messenger of God (2 Corinthians 4:1, 2). He does confess that difficult times have come, but they have not been destructive. When he writes, "We are afflicted" (verse 8), he uses a word that sometimes describes the crushing of grain or grapes. But Paul adds quickly, "But not crushed; perplexed (baffled and frustrated), but not driven to despair; persecuted (chased), but not forsaken; struck down, but not destroyed" (verses 8, 9, RSV).

Paul and other Christians were sometimes at their wits' end, but never at their hope's end. There were times when they felt they had come to a dead end or a rock wall with no room to turn around; but there was never a time when they could not hear the rumbling of the bulldozer on the other side of the wall making a new opening.

Progress in Fellowship

Through difficult situations we gain something of God's perspective and can better manifest God's patience and kindness to others. We become better equipped to share God's kind of comfort with others in their difficult times, because we understand what they are thinking and feeling. We have walked with trust in God through similar situations, and can guide them as well as sympathize. This also gives us added strength.

Paul confessed that God is the God of all comfort, "who comforts us in all our affliction, so that we may be able to comfort those who are in any affliction, with the comfort with which we ourselves are comforted by God" (2 Corinthians 1:4, RSV). In fact, he said, "If we are afflicted, it is for your comfort" (1:6, RSV). The ability to comfort people is a gift God gives to some Christians. For some, it comes through the handling of difficult times triumphantly.

What an insight! We Christians are connected to each other, for the church is a body. There is a "domino" effect within Christianity. The attitudes and activities of one person can spread like cancer. A little leaven leavens a whole lump. Have you noticed how quickly defeatist and negative attitudes spread? Some people are stopped by these poisonous attitudes and are not equipped to handle the difficulties of life.

Victorious, positive, and optimistic attitudes can spread also. These equip a person to be triumphant in difficulty. How do such attitudes spread? By our actions and our speech. But we won't have much victory to spread unless we have gone through some battles ourselves. The church needs those who with faith have conquered whatever threatened them. Some of the greatest people of God have been some of those little people who have walked with Him through difficult times. Their examples of triumphant faith can minister to us.

Progress in Humility

God also can use difficult circumstances to humble us and help us to depend upon Him. Paul sensed that he needed such dependence, and I suspect we do also (2 Corinthians 1:9; 12:9, 10). It is easy to think things are getting done just because of *me*.

In the midst of prosperity, it is easy to think, "Who needs God? I can make it alone." If we get hungry, we can go to the supermarket. If we get sick, we can go to the doctor. If we lose our jobs, we can get unemployment checks. When those run out, we can go on welfare. If a tornado hits our home, we have insurance. If the insurance does not cover it all, we can go to the loan companies. When we grow old, there will be social security and pensions. We can even arrange our own funerals. So who needs God? Such pride, arrogance, and autonomy are damaging to ourselves and to the society in which we live. We need to have times in which there is no one else to turn to but God, so that these selfish qualities will be curbed, and dependence on God will be cultivated.

Progress in Hope

In discussing difficult times, Peter said, "Blessed be the God and Father of our Lord Jesus Christ, who according to His great mercy has caused us to be born again to a living hope through the resurrection of Jesus Christ from the dead" (1 Peter 1:3, NAS).

Living hope is an active hope. It does not sit around and wring its hands. It is based on evidence. Fact produces hope, and hope produces action. For instance, when you receive word that relatives are coming to visit, hope results in preparatory activity—cleaning the house, arranging the menus, and planning activities.

It is the same with our Christian hope. The resurrection is evidence that God can be victorious in tragedies, however bad they may appear. If God can bring victory out of the cross, He can be victorious in any situation. So Christians do not sit around and worry, but they plan and work for Christ.

Victory or Defeat

While Satan can use difficult circumstances to turn us from God, God can use them to turn us to Him. There are many ways that good can come out of troubles, but we cannot always decide in advance what good will come. Sometimes we cannot see what the good is, even while we are receiving it. What we can do is to trust that God, who has always kept His promises, will continue to do so whether we recognize it or not. When we do realize what good has come out of a trying situation, let us then testify about it and give God the glory. God has promised to make good come out of every circumstance. Remember, however, that the promise is not for everyone, but just for those who love God. For others, troublesome circumstances can cause them to turn away from God, not to Him. They can resort to criticism, not to comfort. Trials can destroy character, not build it.

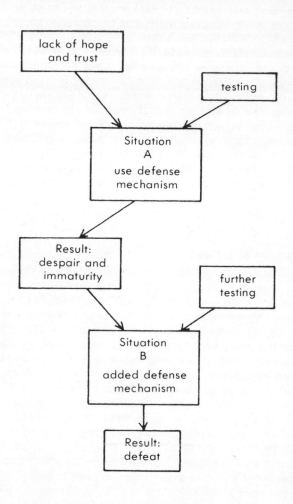

ROUTE OF VICTORY

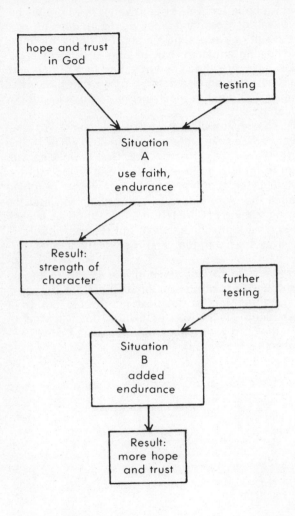

Whether we are victorious or defeated in life depends on what we hope for (pleasure or character), how we hope (actively or passively), in whom we believe (self or God), and what we do (endure or exit). The result of one testing situation is poured into the next testing situation. Out of one situation we can either have more hope and trust and love to pour into the next situation (for victory), or we can have more despair and defense mechanisms to pour into it (for defeat).

Of course, troublesome times will come. We shall never be free from suffering and testing while on this earth. We should remember that God is working with them to bring a good result. Remember too that the sufferings of the present are not worth weighing against the glory that is to be revealed to us at the second coming of Christ (Romans 8:18). Jesus himself faced what looked like defeat, but He was victorious. Our lives are hid in Him, and His victory is ours.

Thanks be to God, who gives us the victory through our Lord Jesus Christ. Therefore, my beloved brethren, be steadfast, immovable, always abounding in the work of the Lord, knowing that in the Lord your labor is not in vain (1 Corinthians 15:57, 58, RSV).

God's Will and Our Prosperity

If God is not the direct cause of all our problems and suffering, although He allows them, then is He the direct cause of all our prosperity? "God wants you to be rich" is becoming a popular slogan. The idea is that if you are really pleasing God by doing His will, He will bless you with earthly prosperity. To say it another way, God will pay you for being good. You can estimate your spiritual account by your earthly savings account.

If that idea is true, then Jesus was a colossal flop! He himself admitted that birds and foxes had more earthly property than He had (Luke 9:58). He looked to a fish for financial resources to pay His taxes (Matthew 17:24-27). Other people paid for His food and lodging (Luke 8:1-3). For a man in His thirties, He was certainly not the *Wall Street Journal's* picture of success.

If living out God's will is demonstrated by leaving a big estate to one's descendants, then Paul stepped outside God's will when he became a Christian. Often He had no food, no drink, no comfortable lodging (2

89

Corinthians 11:27). If Paul was in hunger and in want, it is not true that our earthly needs will always be met abundantly if we are doing God's will (Philippians 4:12).

These examples of Jesus and Paul could cause us to glorify poverty and condemn prosperity, but we are not to do that either. We must be careful about criticizing the rich, for no one is richer than God. We have spent much time in the preceding chapters discussing how we are to understand and handle our problems and sufferings. But how are we to understand and handle our prosperity?

The Source of Prosperity

Prosperity is not the direct blessing of God automatically rewarding man's righteousness. Some prosperity is the result of others' investments and work, not ours. A person cannot pat himself on the back when he is the heir of someone else's wealth; this type of prosperity sometimes falls upon those who have no concern for God.

Some prosperity comes from unrighteous acts. Sin often has a big payroll. Some of those who deal in pornography are becoming exceedingly wealthy. The Mafia is not known for its poverty. Evidently Zacchaeus had become wealthy by cheating others (Luke 19:2, 8). At least a portion of Simon's bank account was evidently the result of exploitation of naive people (Acts 8:9-11). Some people have won a million dollars in state lotteries. Satan knows how to lure people by riches. He even used that bait with Jesus: "All these things will I give You, if You fall down and worship me" (Matthew 4:9, NAS).

Some prosperity is the result of national circumstances. We in the United States are experiencing this. We came out of a great depression into the second World War, which opened factories. After the war, we became a consumer's nation for the first time in two decades. The atmosphere was (and still is) charged with consumerism, encouraged by a new device—television.

Some prosperity is the result of nature itself. Snow falling at the right time and in the right place can make a ski resort very prosperous. The right combination of sun and rain can make bumper crops possible. But we must remember that God sends the sun and rain to both the righteous and the unrighteous (Matthew 5:45). A pagan farmer can be just as materially rich as his godly neighbor.

Even a natural disaster can bring prosperity to some. A tornado can help builders and suppliers. Some crops being wiped out in one area can help those who have good crops in another area.

Some prosperity comes from being in the right place at the right time. An oil boom is one example. Some prosperity comes from our economic environment. The rise in real-estate values has made some people millionaires. Wise investments cause many to prosper whether they are righteous or not.

And, of course, some prosperity comes to godly people who have given God the priority in their stewardship of their whole lives. I know several Christians whose wealth is the result of putting God first, but usually other circumstances are coupled with that commitment.

God allows prosperity, but He does not always directly cause it as a reward for our being good. However, both He and Satan want to control the way we *handle* prosperity.

Handling Prosperity

Prosperous is a very relative term. Most of us think of people more wealthy than we when the term is mentioned. But there are poorer people who think of us as prosperous. Therefore being able to handle prosperity is a concern for each of us. Mature responsibility requires both proper attitudes and proper activities.

Faith. The person who has become prosperous without God may easily conclude that he does not need God. A Christian who can trace the source of his prosperity to some of the circumstances we discussed earlier may also begin to feel he is self-sufficient. It is easy to think, "I've done it all."

But mature Christian thinking understands that God is both the Creator and the owner of everything. Since He is eternal, we trust that His way also is eternal—lasting forever. Therefore we move our trust from *what* we own (things that do not last) to *who* owns them (God, who is eternal). The value of our possessions can take a nose dive when the bottom falls out on Wall Street. A tornado, flood, or earthquake can wipe out everything we have, but it can't touch God. An iceberg can put an end to the great Titanic, but it can't faze God. Time can crumble the mountains, but God is eternal.

Job lived triumphantly through the destruction of his wealth and family because he knew that all things are temporary, while God is eternal. He was the richest man in the East (Job 1:3) who became the poorest overnight. But he trusted the one who owned everything. Life was not hopeless as long as the one who could not be destroyed was still around. Job stubbornly believed in God, not in gadgets. Eventually God blessed Job with more material wealth than he had at the height of his former prosperity (42:12).

Humility. Knowing that everything is continuously deteriorating should humble the rich. Everything we own is passing away. Earthly wealth is not lasting.

So you own a hundred new cars? You own a potential junk yard! James spoke about glorying in our humiliation (James 1:10, 11). We must properly

92

evaluate ourselves and our things in comparison with God, and take no pride either in ourselves or in our prosperity. We must submit to God's greatness and ownership. All we have is His. Everything we own belongs to the "company" God owns. Our clothes are "company" clothes; we live in "company" houses; we drive "company" cars. We have been bought with a price; we are not our own (1 Corinthians 6:19, 20). We are not the executives in the company; we are servants of the company president—God.

Fellowship. Those who are humble even with their riches do not "put on airs." They are happy to associate with the lowly (Romans 12:16). I have seen it happen many times. The rich will sit next to the poor during worship; they eat alongside the poor at the fellowship meal; they eat beans and cornbread; they play on the church's softball team.

These people are entirely different from the Howard Hugheses of our day who become social hermits because of their wealth. A man who gains the whole world but drops out of fellowship can lose not only his senses but also his soul—and then what is the whole world worth to him? (Mark 8:36).

It is not entirely their fault, but many rich people are the loneliest people in the church. Those Christians who are not so wealthy do not voluntarily fellowship with them. The less wealthy feel uncomfortable with the very rich; they do not want anyone to think they are friendly with the rich just because they are rich. Thus the rich people are left to the fellowship of those who really are seeking their favor just because they are rich. How much better it would be if we would invite the rich Christians to our homes, and discover what wonderful brothers and sisters they can be!

Usage. Jesus said it would be difficult for the rich to enter the kingdom of Heaven (Matthew 19:23). Riches can be very deceitful. They can trick us into believing in the wrong values, and worldly cares can strangle the effectiveness of God's Word (Matthew 13:22).

Remember the example of the rich man and Lazarus? One of the richest men could have helped one of the most righteous men, but he refused (Luke 16:19-31). What is important to God is not what we have, but how we use it.

Some people think all riches need to be redistributed, but the Bible does not support that view. It is true that Jesus told one person to sell what he had and give to the poor (Matthew 19:21), but that is not a commandment for all of Jesus' followers. The Master could see that this particular man was making wealth his first priority. To follow Christ, this one would have to give up his earthly possessions in order to transfer his full commitment. Jesus never told Mary and Martha to sell their house. In fact, he enjoyed retreating there (Luke 10:38-42). He told a paralytic and a blind man to go to their homes, not to sell them (Matthew 9:6; Mark 8:26). Some of the early Christians sold some of their property; but not all Christians did so, for we read that they met and fellowshipped in their houses (Acts 2:45, 46; 12:12; Romans 16:5; 1 Corinthians 16:19).

The point is this: our possessions should not detour us from helping others. We do not want our things to become more valuable to us than people. Paul wrote to Timothy some fine advice about the use of riches:

> As for the rich in this world, charge them not to be haughty, nor to set their hopes on uncertain riches but on God who richly furnishes us with everything to enjoy. They are to do good, to be rich in good deeds, liberal and generous, thus laying up for themselves a good foundation for the future, so that they may take hold of the life which is life indeed (1 Timothy 6:17-19, RSV).

In deciding how to use our money, we should follow the principles that we discussed earlier in thinking about how to make decisions within God's will. The Bible gives us some guidance. For instance, Paul tells us not to feed a brother who refuses to work (2 Thessalonians 3:10). This refers, of course, to one who refuses from laziness, not physical inability. We are to care for the poor who really need help (2 Corinthians 8, 9; 1 Corinthians 16:1-4; Proverbs 19:17; 22:2; Matthew 25:31-46). We are to provide for our families (1 Timothy 5:1-16) and for the preaching of God's Word (1 Corinthians 9:14). Paul also made clear that we are not to sue one another to gain wealth (1 Corinthians 6:1-8).

Some people have more money than maturity, and therefore counsel is important. There are many hands stretched out for the Christian's dollars. Not all who ask are worthy; some people are out to "fleece" God's sheep. We must seek counsel and use common sense. We must investigate the background and character of people who ask us to support their various ministries. I doubt very much that Paul would advise others to support the ministry of Hymenaeus and Alexander (1 Timothy 1:20). I would also think twice before making a contribution to someone who said he had a vision that I would give him a certain amount of money.

Neither is it always wise to spend or give away all the money we have; it may be wiser to use part of it in ways that will gain a profit so there will be more to use. Jesus made this principle clear in the parable of the talents. He commended those who made wise investments (Matthew 25:14-30).

Some feel it is wrong for a church to have any money in a savings account. We really don't have a clear "thus saith the Lord" on that issue. In my judgment, the answer lies in the attitude of the church. Does that savings account own the people, or do they

95

own it? If it prevents a church from serving, then Jesus' advice to the rich young ruler probably applies (Matthew 19:21). Anything that prevents us from being unselfish must go.

I know of a church that inherited over two hundred thousand dollars. They put it into a savings account and decided not to touch it. They would not even loan some to a sister congregation at less than the commercial interest rate, though repayment would have been no problem. They could have used that money to help both churches, but the inheritance owned them. Many times money can destroy the Christlike sharing of an individual or a group. Christ knew what He was saying when He spoke of the deceitfulness of riches. Any investment or prosperity should enhance our ability to serve.

Conclusion

Although our prosperity may not be the direct result of God's rewarding us for righteousness, it can be a direct source of our serving Him in righteousness. May we do so with trust that God, who supplies seed to the sower, will continue to supply and multiply our seed for sowing, so that the usage of our riches will result in a harvest of righteousness (2 Corinthians 9:10). In that way we will glorify God (verse 13) and cause more people to lift up their prayers in thanksgiving to Him (verses 12, 14). We will not only be doing the will of God, but also spreading the understanding of His will to others. Let us pray and let us live with our prosperity in this commitment: "Not my will, but thine, be done."